Releasement

D1716062

RELEASEMENT

Spirituality for Ministry

Barbara Fiand

CROSSROAD·NEW YORK

1993

The Crossroad Publishing Company
370 Lexington Avenue, New York, N.Y. 10017

Printed in the United States of America

Library of Congress Cataloging in Publication Data

Fiand, Barbara.
    Releasement : spirituality for ministry.

    1. Spiritual life—Catholic authors.   2. Clergy—
Office.   3. Church work.   4. Monastic and religious
life.   I. Title
BX2350.2.F46   1987   248.4'8209   87-2541
ISBN 0-8245-1083-6

Acknowledgments

Four of the chapters of this book have appeared previously in earlier
versions: "Ministering toward Thought" in *Review for Religious* 40/6
(1981); "The Appropriation of Freedom," under the title "Liberty: A
Nonpolitical Reflection," in *Soundings* 63/3 (1980); "Toward Solidarity
with the Poor" in a bulletin published by the Religious Formation
Conference (1984); and "Prayer as Listening: A Practical Approach"
in *Diakonia* 16/3 (1981)

To Julie Billiart,
a woman who knew
how to love

Contents

Foreword

Contemplation is the ability to see the presence of God in the world around us, to recognize the face of Christ in the face of the sister and the brother, to develop a whole new way of looking at things. That is why without it good works can at best be only good works. It is up to the contemplative to bring a sense of the sacred onto the scene, not just simply a sense of the system. To view the world with a contemplative vision is to see the world as Jesus sees it.

To lead an efficient, distanced, and almost frenetic society from fascination with action to concern for meanings and implications could well be the final great gift of the church to this time. Without it we may certainly perish in both soul and in body at the hands of the systems we have made.

Releasement challenges each of us to look at the soul behind the systems in which we find ourselves. It links once more the contemplative and the concrete, too long now made to be natural enemies instead of necessary partners. It makes philosophy our most pragmatic of lost subjects.

With the rise of individualism and specialization in the Western world came a kind of schizophrenic separation of body and soul, ends and means, beauty and truth. We distinguish now, with great facility, between the legal and the moral, the doable and the desirable, the regrettable and the essential. We can't think anymore about what is right when we are surrounded by what is possible. Few ask whether what is possible is also morally appropriate. And those who do ask are dismissed with supercilious smiles.

It is time for us to begin to put our splintered selves back together again. We must learn to think thankfully, to repent, to care about things larger than ourselves, to see the segments as simply symptoms of the whole, to develop a global vision based on a universal view.

But to do that we will have to begin to bring soul to skill, and vision to need.

This book, I believe, helps us make that new beginning beyond skills and boundaries to Gospel breadth. It shows us that good will is not enough, professionalism is not enough, activity is not enough. To do something special we must each be something special.

The world has never needed the true contemplative more.

Sister Joan D. Chittister, O.S.B.

Preface

The meditations that make up this book were presented separately over a number of years: some as essays published in a number of different journals; others as talks given at various workshops and retreats. They are connected, therefore, not by the time and occasion of authorship or delivery; nor are they now in collected form because of any commitment on my part to develop one particular theme systematically throughout this work. Their collection must rather be attributed to a common concern present in each essay and expressive of the life journey of the author. It is a concern to explore the ground, the basis, or perhaps better stated, the depth dimension of human existence; a concern to touch the fundamental disposition necessary for effective ministry. This disposition needs to be prior to all action and is a prerequisite for personal wholeness and integrity, a disposition identified in this work by the Eckhartian term *releasement*.[1]

During the last several years of teaching men and women in training for both ordained and lay ministry, I have become increasingly aware of the need to move beyond the "how-to" manuals, toward reflection on depth, on attitude, on fundamental stance. We are pilgrims. Our home is the heart of God. Each chapter's reflection addresses itself either directly or indirectly to this issue. Holiness, it is suggested over and over again, means *releasement toward wholeness*: creative surrender to the mystery which works itself out in the brokenness and the healing, the agony and the joy of our lives.

We live in an age of extroversion. Active participation in the community; the *doing* of justice in work and word; the bearing of visible fruits as evidence that something is "going on" are all valued highly. Whether we are conscious of it or not, we want to touch and to *see* the presence of the Kingdom. We suspect that which is hidden and intangible, and often find ourselves impatient with what seems to have already taken "too long." Pious abstractions quite clearly will not do any longer. An urgency overwhelms us as we face our own personal responsibility for the mission of Jesus. With the psalmist (Ps. 13) we want to cry out: "How long, O God? . . . How long? . . . "

It seems to me that all of this is as it should be. It is imperative for our times that we be concerned. Religion as a tranquilizer is simply no longer accepted as part (nor was it ever *truly* a part) of the message of the One who came to bring fire upon the earth and was consumed with zeal for its kindling (Luke 12:49). Today, more perhaps than ever before, the word is *involvement*. Being in the world, feeling its pain, and joining the ranks of those working on behalf of justice are authentic signs of vocation. Where then is there room for a book concerned with holiness, with releasement, which urges the contemporary Christian toward *thought*? Is not this a luxury reserved for ivory towers, for men and women of leisure? We hear in these pages of "letting-be," of creative surrender, of the value of pain. What does all this have to do with justice, with building the Kingdom? It is hoped that for the earnest reader of this book the answer to these questions will not be long in coming.

The first chapter ought to shatter any illusion or apprehension about quietism and irresponsible tranquility. Thinking is there identified as the necessary means toward recognizing *authentic* interdependence and, thus, toward opening us up to reverential coexistence. Authentic thoughtfulness allows for creative acceptance of the differences which constitute the human community. It furthers uniqueness while fostering reverential at-oneness with others. The ministry toward thought (sadly neglected in our time) is presented as the prerequisite for all other ministries on behalf of justice, for it undercuts the Will to Power and, by exposing us to our own vulnerability, opens us up to each other in gratitude.

The first chapter, then, sets the stage, if you will, for a probing of attitudes which continues throughout the other seven chapters; it is offered as a necessary complement to the extroversion and activity to which we are driven by our culture and by the needs of our time. We all know that a minister is not a machine carrying out assigned tasks. His/her service is *grounded* in a disposition and must be rooted in inwardness. The neglect of the latter makes Christian service shallow, a mere "job" devoid of creative energy and fire. The influence of Christian tradition and of cultural values and disvalues, which shapes our attitudes, informs our actions, and directs our interests, must be brought to light; it must be examined with deeper awareness, and critically rethought if it is to serve us toward wholeness. There are issues and concerns that address us with particular intensity at our time in history. Although not all of them can be dealt with in this book, I have selected some of the more pressing ones:

- the issue of freedom and its relationship to inner growth;
- the issue of poverty and our call to interiorize our solidarity with the oppressed;
- the mystery of pain and its place in a hedonistic society;
- the relationship between authority and authentic obedience;
- the question of feminine and masculine polarities, of an androgynous ministry which respects diversity while working toward the whole;
- the mandate to pray, to be still, to listen, and to wait in a world where noise and speed seem of the utmost consequence.

Probing and reflecting opens us to the unexpected in our ministry; to the different, the seemingly paradoxical, the unusual, the life-giving. Out of depth comes newness and power. The inner well never runs dry except by lack of use. The issues opened up by these reflections are offered as "ministry toward thought" in the hope of evoking new perspectives. They are offered without pretensions, open-ended, and, therefore, claiming no closure. It is my conviction that there are few if any answers to the ultimate concerns of the human heart — no answers, at least, that can be formulated once and for all. It seems that we stand forever in questions which, upon probing, open up to deeper questions and greater yearning. Our answers lie in the asking, in the thinking, in the journeying.

Notes

1. *Releasement* is chosen as the most meaningful translation of the German word *Gelassenheit*, referring here to Meister Eckhart's concept of *Seinlassen*. In his many works on Eckhart, Matthew Fox describes *Seinlassen* as an attitude of "letting be," the fruit of a prior having "let go." It is seen by Eckhart as a dimension of *Abgeschiedenheit*, a virginal state of being or a state of empty openness which yearns to bear fruit, to become impregnated and to give forth life. In the present work I have chosen the title *Releasement* to embrace both the attitude of "letting be" and of "letting go" simultaneously pointing to a singular movement of the spirit which in freeing itself sets free, in emptying itself empowers, in letting go (being increasingly released from bondage) lets others be and releases them ever more into freedom, hence authentically ministering to them.

1

Ministering toward Thought

In our days much consideration is being given to broadening our understanding of ministry. We use the term when we work with the poor, the elderly, youth. Our "ministries" extend to the handicapped in mind and body, to migrant workers, to aliens, to minorities, to oppressed persons of every kind. We "minister" as we speak out for justice; as we put ourselves in the forefront of the battles for equality and for rights; as we lobby; as we demonstrate and remonstrate; as we stand for truth and for freedom. Much has been given us. We are reminded of our stewardship: s/he who has received much must give in return — must minister — must share the gifts.

Most of us eagerly respond to the challenge. Generosity does not seem to be lacking. Men and women ministers for the most part know that they have been touched by love and surrender creatively in whatever manner seems most fitting to them. Ours is an age of great needs and the calls to service for each one of us are undoubtedly manifold. It seems almost pretentious, therefore, on my part to explore yet another area where our help is desperately needed; I would, indeed, make no such attempt were I not convinced that what I have called "ministering toward thought" is an essential aspect of all our already existing ministries.

But what does it mean to "minister toward thought"? Are not all of us human and therefore rational creatures? Is not thinking natural to everyone, and have not we, particularly in the

Western technological world, sufficient evidence of the power of the mind? Most psychologists concerned with our humanness would probably tell us that thinking hàs in fact been exercised too much in our age and that, as a result, the other human potential called *feeling* has virtually atrophied. What business have we then to minister toward thought? Perhaps it would be wiser, and more in line with human rights, were we to minister toward authentic feeling.

The issue, of course, revolves around the meaning of *thinking*. It is clear that one must distinguish between thought and logical analysis and synthesis. The arduous task of working from premise to conclusion or even of dissecting the premise and analyzing content, valuable though it may be, is not what is meant here by "thought." Thought, understood fundamentally, precedes and transcends analysis and synthesis. It is primary both in the sense of "coming before," and in the sense of containing—holding and, therefore, surpassing either one of these methods of reasoning.

To minister toward thought, therefore, does not mean to reason effectively and to help others to do so. This would be a praiseworthy, though limited, ministry. It would pertain primarily to teachers, and most likely to philosophers and mathematicians among them. The ministry that we are discussing is much more universal.

Thinking as Thanking

But what is meant by *thought*, and how is it that we are universally called to minister "toward" it? Martin Heidegger, the philosopher of thought-fulness, leads us to trace the roots of the word *thinking* to the Old English *Thanc*[1] (German *Dank*), and thus very effectively relates *thinking* to *thanking*; thought to thank-fulness. I am thank-ful when I am conscious of having been gifted. Giftedness becomes creative only to the extent to which I have *received* what has been *freely given*. There is in thankfulness, it seems, a receptivity which is at the same time a response. When I am grateful, I am, as it were, creatively passive: I am opened to receive and to give. I am *released*: freed *from* the fetters of my own false sense of independence, *toward* that gentle admission of interdependence, which opens up to the other as giver, and gives to him/her my receptivity as gift.

Releasement, which constitutes my thinking as thanking, is openness to my being-together-with-others-in-the-world. It is a fundamental letting-be, in which I experience myself existentially as reverential openness to everything that is, as freedom which, in turn, frees all things by allowing them to reveal, to give themselves to me *as they are*.

Undoubtedly for many of us, accustomed as we are to the technological world view and, therefore, to thinking as "acting upon" reality rather than "receiving from" it, the above interpretation will, at best, sound strange. Is it not true, however, that even in the most elementary sense, consciousness of implies openness to? Humankind differentiates itself from the animal and from matter in general precisely because of a certain translucency whereby *meaning* is received and passed on to others. Aristotle long ago made it quite plain that in terms of our relation to this world nothing is in the mind that did not first pass through the senses. The senses, he claimed, were our channels of receptivity. *Thinking* as receptive-response is clearly not a *new*, though today it may be a forgotten, concept. It would seem that a reverential return to the roots of language opens for us depths far beyond the shallow interpretations to which modern usage has reduced it.

Thinking, then, must be seen as thanking; thought as thankfulness; and ministry toward thought as empowerment toward gratitude. How precisely are we to understand all this? Above, we identified authentic thinking with releasement and saw the latter as openness to what might be called "cobeing": creative presence to the other with whom I am in this world. Releasement, more precisely, is freedom from preconception, prejudgments (which always constrict my vision). It is openness to what is *as it is*. As such it is openness to reality as gift. It receives without preconditions. In its receptivity it *gives* because it lets-be. In letting-be it empowers. Ministering toward thought as releasement, therefore, is ministering toward empowerment, toward freedom.

More concretely understood, this empowering of all creation to be what it is, can be seen as a creative *yes* to the different; as such, serving authentic dialogue and furthering growth. Authentic dialogue gathers the different *as* different and holds it in creative tension. It is not afraid of meaningful confrontation, nor threatened by dissent. Its unity is found not in conformity but precisely in that diversity which, because it holds its own, allows the other to be.

Thankful thoughtfulness allows us to see that the treasure of our very uniqueness, our individuality, can be safeguarded *only* if and when we allow the other to be other. Its gratitude receives the other in his/her difference as an affirmation of personal unrepeatability. Its creative response (authentic dialogue) works toward unity in diversity.

Releasement: A Mystical Interpretation

Within the religious dimension we can see the call toward thankful-thoughtfulness, toward releasement, at its profoundest in the writings of the mystics. Eckhart, for one, interprets the creation of humankind as primarily and fundamentally a *call* toward releasement. He, like other mystics, sees creation in its multiplicity and diversity as reflecting the oneness of God.[2] It is clear that multiplicity is intelligible only within the context of unity. The word *uni-verse* expresses this most eloquently, implying as it does a oneness in the manifold: "to turn into one." The person, says Eckhart, is the one called to give voice to all this;

to find and then to articulate the meaning of the different as it is held in unity. Inasmuch as we *think*, we hold all things in their significance. Things in themselves are blind. They find their openness and are held together in us as persons.

Eckhart interprets this event of our receptive responsiveness to creation as our primordial call to what he calls "virgin motherhood." Into our openness, he says, God sends His/Her silent, overwhelming presence. We become the *there*, the place, the home for this presence. God acts, and we are actualized; we become. Our openness, of course, is not primary to God's work. His/Her creative presence in us actualizes our openness, our presence to Him/Her.

For Eckhart God's self-sending is best symbolized by way of a mirror image:[3] The mirror receives its being, as we know, *by mirroring*. Without the countenance gazing into it, it *is* nothing. Thus gazing into the mirror brings the mirror *as* mirror into being while, at the same time, it ceases to be noticed, since the person gazing into it is absorbed only in his/her countenance. *The being in the mirror, therefore, is the being of the mirrored. That which makes the mirror image what it is is the countenance reflected in the mirror, not the mirror image on its own.* The mirror image and the mirrored image are the same, though they are different. The mirror image gives itself to the one who looks at it and whom it mirrors. The mirror image does not only come from its "other," receiving its being from the "other," it also directs itself toward its "other" and is what it is *for* its "other."

Eckhart tells us that as virgin souls we are called to be like this mirror: to become the silent place of God's presence so that in our releasement nothing other remains in us. We receive our being from God. Our being is God's presence. We thus are Son to God — the ones who *from* God are what we are and nothing else: "Where the Father bears his Son in me," says Eckhart, "there am I the same Son and not another."[4]

It is in our *self*-forgetfulness as virgin souls that we lose ourselves and become the open mirror where God beholds His/

Her countenance, His/Her Son. As virgin souls we are pure presence of the mystery. It is in our openness, our *there*, that the other which we are as human, can become one with God. But it is not sufficient to be a virgin soul. A virgin must receive the seed and bear fruit. All of us are meant to be mothers, says the mystic. We are called to be mothers of God. It is in the gratitude of love, which we as virgin souls experience in our becoming, that we bear fruit. Gratitude is a movement from the one who receives to the one who gives. It echoes the goodness of the giver and returns to him/her. The giver shines forth from the one who receives in gratitude. The act of giving into the grateful soul, thus, allows fruit to be born. God gives Him/Herself and receives Him/Herself back in the virgin soul who becomes *mother* in *thanks-giving*.

> The fruitfulness of the gift, that alone is gratitude for the gift, and thus the spirit becomes mother in the re-birth of gratitude, since s/he bears Jesus again into the heart of the Father.[5]

The virgin soul, sunk in inwardness, is one with God. In our inwardness we receive God and become His/Her image. We become, through gratitude, the living reflection, echo, of God. It is here that our fulfillment lies. It is in this, our virginal motherhood, that we are truly free, because, in our total openness, we see the being of all beings flow continuously from the divine abyss. Creation is "nothing" of itself—its being is a constant flow outward from God, whose nature is *giving*. This flow outward receives its affirmation in our virgin mothering, because, as human, we can articulate it, and as virgin, we are released toward it.

Liberated from all preconceptions about things, we can embrace them; we can let them *be*. We are opened up to wonder, because we are free from the prison of determinations and opened to the mystery. Things no longer possess us. We stand "near them but not in them." We are care-ful with things as everything is the gathering place of God.

As virgin mothers, in the true spirit of poverty, we order all things according to the divine light wherein we now see everything. The eternal calls us. We are no longer obsessed with manipulation, productivity, calculation, verification. We are released as we gaze at all things not merely *as objects*, for they no longer reveal themselves primarily as such, but rather point beyond themselves to the ground from which everything comes and to which all things return.

The secret lies in letting things *be* what they *are* — "wood as wood," "mountains as mountains," "water as water." In the freedom thus granted them, they reveal the mystery within. "Blessed are they who have eyes to see." These are the eyes of freedom.

Sin as the Will to Power

Eckhart sees sin as the refusal to articulate the oneness in diversity which is God. It is a refusal to think, a refusal to be released. In sin I will my *own oneness* instead of the oneness in God; I destroy harmony. In the will-ful attempt to be *one* with all beings, I run the risk of wishing to make *their* difference into my one-ness, reducing them to a finite unity — my own. Thus I lack releasement. I violate their *difference* which, in its difference alone, is authentically one with me. Hence I destroy rather than build. The destruction lies in my will. I am afraid to surrender, to give up control. In this is the root of all evil.[6]

Eckhart explains the above as follows: to become who I am I must surrender to the other, take a risk, be released and release. This frightens me and I shrink from it; but I can only shrink into myself, my finitude. This, however, is never enough for me for, as was said above, I am marked from the moment of my creation by the infinite — called to be the image of God; to hold the universe in oneness and articulate its splendor; to mother it back to God; to build the Kingdom. In the dissatisfaction created by my refusal to surrender, I tend to absolutize my own finite will in order to make up for the lack brought about by my unfaithfulness to the call of my being.[7] Absolutizing myself, of course, is the *Will to Power*. In it is the sin of the world. By it I destroy the other and (given the above interpretation of releasement) I also destroy myself.

Practical Application

One might at this point wonder whether the ministry toward thought will not need a more practical dimension than the realm of the mystical in order to be credible. Mystical thought, however, is an essential element of every authentically religious interpretation of ministry; for through its radical God-centeredness it roots religious action in its source.

Practical applications for the ministry toward thought are, of course, not difficult to find. In the Western world, particularly, the need for releasement — the creative *yes* to the different — is epidemic. Ours *is* the age of the Will to Power. The movement toward conformity, not only in externals but even in our innermost thoughts, is no longer a matter of personal choice. Through mass communication, endless repetition of slogans, ostracization of dissenters, and public censures (subtle though these may be) of anyone who dares to be different, it has today become a force that threatens even the staunchest individual. The slogan "in unity there is strength" is unquestioningly accepted, but the thoughtful understanding of *unity* as deriving authentic power only through a reverential acceptance of the diversity which constitutes the oneness is often sadly lacking.

How is it that in the land of the brave and the free an appreciation of freedom as the *right* to be different is so blatantly absent? Are not the cultural minorities in our country the most poignant examples of our pathetic failure, thus far, to be truly released? What is culture, however, if it is not the loving affirmation of my at-oneness with some and difference from others in the interpretation of beauty, truth, and goodness? That this interpretation contains within itself the dialectical possibility of its opposite is obvious. Human beings are finite. Who has an edge on truth, on beauty, and on authentic goodness? Is not the acceptance of the different, particularly in this domain, enriching, edifying? "One nation under God, indivisible, with liberty and justice for all."

But need we in our ministry toward releasement restrict our vision to international or even national needs? What of our own communities, local organizations, interpersonal relationships? How is it with our personal gratitude: the releasement with which we encounter the different ones among us? What of the neighbor who voted for a different party; the son who wants to work instead of going to college? What about the ordained or vowed minister I work or live with whose interpretation of prayer and action, of the charism of the community, of religious decorum or dress, differs from mine? How do I see the priest whose style of worship is different from mine, or the person in the back pew of my church who continues to pray privately during public worship. What about those who dissent? Do I see their difference as a threat to me — a condemnation or criticism of myself? Do I see disagreement as attack? Can I dialogue with persons who do not see my way even if it means that our agreement will be an acceptance of our disagreement? Does the difference of others free me to be who I am, or awaken my sleeping insecurities about myself and arouse my indignation? How does it stand with my own thought-fulness and my ministry to myself in this regard?

It should, at this point, not be too difficult to see why, at the beginning of this reflection, the ministry toward thought was identified as an essential aspect of *all* our already existing ministries. When we work in the service of thought-ful releasement, we work toward the openness of all to all. "Father, that they may be one in us even as you are in me and I am in you" (John 17:21). This means that we work toward the Kingdom in the most fundamental sense. We can now more clearly identify why a correct understanding of this ministry calls us primarily toward ministering to our inmost selves. "The Kingdom of God is within," and accepts the mystical (which, after all, is nothing more than a *personal* encounter with the divine) as an authentic interpretation of things.

Heidegger somberly points out that ours is the age of thought-lessness. The most thought-provoking fact in these our thought-poor times, he says, is that we have not as yet learned how to think.[8]

But what about a concrete suggestion for ministry in this regard? How do we truly *work* toward a furtherance of thankful openness to the different? We can do so only by witnessing to it ourselves. Thinking that thanks is gratitude that frees us into vulnerability, into releasement into oneness and toward God. As we stand in releasement we release, we empower. By our own vulnerability we set free. What greater mission is there? Our gift to others is our grateful acceptance of them as they are, in humility and in love. We receive their gift out of a genuine sense of our own poverty and need of them as different from us. In our acceptance of them we affirm and we are affirmed; thus we minister and are ministered to. In giving we are gifted; thus in creative openness we articulate our oneness in God.

Notes

1. Martin Heidegger, *What Is Called Thinking?* trans. Fred. W. Wiek and J. Glenn Gray (New York: Harper Torch Books, 1972), p. 139.

2. Bernhard Welte, *Meister Eckhart* (Freiburg: Herder, 1979), pp. 183, 210, 211.

3. Josef Quint, ed., *Meister Eckhart, Deutsche Predigten und Traktate* (Munich: Carl Hanser Verlag, 1963), pp. 224–28, Sermon 16. An

explication of the main thought expressed in this sermon was taken from Welte, *Meister Eckhart*, pp. 126–39.

4. Welte, *Meister Eckhart*, p. 131 (translation mine).

5. Ibid., p. 134 (translation mine).

6. Ibid., pp. 223, 224.

7. Ibid., p. 225.

8. Martin Heidegger, *Vorträge und Aufsätze*, 3 vols., 3rd ed. (Pfullingen: Verlag Günther Neske, 1969), 2:5.

2

The Appropriation of Freedom

Freedom is essential to human dignity; it is inviolable and sacred — these are affirmations of our Western democratic beliefs. Our Constitution guarantees and safeguards freedom of speech as well as action. It remains questionable, however, whether this treasure which is our heritage, in defense of which men go to war and die, in protection of which government is established and maintained by free elections, ever means more to us than the *liberty to act as we think best*.

Ours is the age when action rules supreme. A person is judged by his/her achievements or potential for achievement. What we can do is quantitatively evaluated, and equality between the races as between the sexes is measured in terms of opportunity for employment: tangible evidence of our capacity to act as the other can act and to make as much money as the other can make.

Our Constitution guarantees us life, liberty, and the pursuit of happiness, and yet alienation and strife tear at our country. The streets of our cities are not safe to walk, and our windows and doors are barred against intruders. If we have the freedom to act as we think best, why is it that happiness is so difficult to achieve? The obvious answer seems to be that we work at cross purposes, one acting to the other's detriment and for his/her own advantage with the strongest one winning. But does this make sense? If the liberty to *act* as we *think* best defines the freedom guaranteed us by the society in which we live, then *should* not the pursuit of happiness be a tangible possibility flowing from this primary right? Persons must be alive to be free and need freedom to be happy: life, liberty, happiness is the distinct order by which these rights are ours as fundamental. How is it then that our prized liberty gives such imperfect evidence of its ability to support happiness?

Perhaps the answer lies in the possibility that in our proclamations of freedom we are suffering a basic misapprehension concerning the *foundation* of this right. To begin with, it might be asked what "liberty to act as one *thinks* right" means; that is, we might be invited to reflect once more upon *thinking*. It is true that even today we are admonished to *think before we act*, and told that abuses will set in unless we do so. From having made this observation, however, it seems a rather short step to the assumption that this is, of course, exactly what every "mature" person does; hence we hold mature persons responsible for their actions. Responsibility, we suggest, is part of the fundamental right to be free. With this we are back to where we started: a person's right (responsibility) to act as s/he thinks best. But what have we learned about thinking?

We noted in our previous reflection that authentic thinking is an attitude: a state of grateful attention directed toward everything that is; a gratitude that springs from the recognition of one's own being as the place where consciousness breaks forth; where the immanence that holds all of nature in a state of sleepy abandonment to itself emerges into transcendence, into a conscious yes to reality. Thinking means to accept gratefully *what* I find, when I find it (conscious awareness of the world about me), and to shape it creatively toward the future. It is a letting-be of what is, which, in its letting-be, creates. It is releasement. It is freedom, freeing itself and everything that is toward authentic Being. What does this mean?

In the previous chapter I identified thinking with releasement: that disposition in which we are held and through which we hold all things in creative abandon, and which lets all things be truly what they are and resists the temptation of restraining things, all living beings, and persons in particular, by categorizing them into preconceived concepts, imposing limits on them.

It would seem that one can impose limits, deny releasement, in two ways: either by neglect or by excessive demands. Our neglect of things prevents them from being what they are meant to be. Our indifference causes them to break. In the same way, of course, our neglect of people — the old, the sick, the lonely, the young — causes them to "break." They die, either physically or spiritually, since they are not encouraged to be, are not "released" by the community which is vital to their existence. (A person is essentially cobeing.)

Denying releasement by making excessive demands on things is an abuse of them in a different fashion: one expects them to perform in a way not designed for them. Hence one destroys them. This attitude as a violation possible also in the sphere of the personal is obvious: an overdemanding relationship is destructive by definition. Releasement in this regard, however, can also be lacking toward oneself, and here the violation of freedom goes unnoticed most often. We are impatient with our own infirmities. The one-sided interpretation of freedom as potentiality for action prevalent today brings with it the implication (quite often unuttered because unthought) of boundlessness. The Will to Power with which action-oriented freedom is inevitably identified cannot but lead to impatience with one's own finitude. The god of independence reigns supreme and need of others is considered as immaturity, as a limitation to be transcended, to be discarded. Mixed together in many of us is a not wanting to need and yet the uncomfortable recognition that we do. Releasement here is surrender to the fact. It is the maturity of accepting interdependence as a given, and of embracing our sisters and brothers *in gratitude for being needed by us*.

It should be clear at this point that the yes which gratefully

embraces reality and which, according to Heidegger, constitutes thinking as thanking — releasement — is indeed the yes of
freedom. It should be equally clear, however, that freedom as
releasement is far from the action-oriented liberty by which we
so frequently interpret this democratic right. We might now
suggest that our right to the freedom of releasement is not ours
because it appears in the Constitution; rather, it is constitutional because it is ours. It is ours because we are, quite simply,
called to releasement; because our nature, as it were, demands
that we achieve this freedom and has us pursue it quite inde-
pendent of "willed" activity — indeed, often in spite of it. But
how does this come about?

At the risk of resurrecting a word which for many a "liberated" thinker might best be left in mothballs, where modern
thought has relegated it, I propose that the freedom of releasement, freedom as a state of being, thought-ful freedom, is ours
only by virtue of our finitude, and can be authentically appro-
priated only through the arduous path of what can be termed
"repentance."

On Repentance

As we know, much has been said about repentance in the past.
Retreats have been preached; treatises written. Persons have
been called from sin to penance and to a renewed form of life.
The fear of God and the dread of rejection from the community
have reformed many lives. But what is authentic repentance in
the context of this reflection? If one confesses one's sins, begs
forgiveness, and chastises the body into submission, does one
repent? Is repentance a turning from sin, a rejection of the
wrong and striving after perfection, or must it, in order to lead
to freedom, be understood at a deeper level?

When, as young persons, we grow from dependence to independence; when we go forth to meet the challenges of life, to

assert ourselves; when we will power in the name of self-fulfill-ment, can we *repent*? Do we even know the meaning of the word? We can undoubtedly experience sorrow for a hurt we have caused, an injustice perpetrated, but have we as yet en-countered ourselves sufficiently to repent?

Let us consider repentance as a *matter of love consummated*: a form of surrender, where sorrow at, and recognition of, one's own limitation is mingled with abandon and surrender to the self *and* to the One who is even deeper than the innermost self, and in whose mercy one trusts. When we are strong we are, it seems, in the throes of the Will to Power, the glories and chal-lenges of existence: "to strive, to seek, to find, and not to yield." The vicissitudes of life encompass us. We bend only to assert ourselves later. We stretch, we plan, we hope. Where is there room to repent? Adventure is a challenge, repentance is surren-der.

In striving, repentance is allowed no room. Strangely, how-ever, it is not totally absent. Its silent presence is already secret-ly with us, for as we experience the pain of our strivings in the hurt of rejection, in the reluctant admission that everything is not always right, the door is already opened to surrender—the surrender, that is, of ourselves to ourselves; the surrender of humility, of gentleness; the surrender of wisdom, of release-ment, of authentic freedom. It announces itself, it seems to me, first with that disquieting recognition that there is *really* no power in the Will to Power; that authentic strength lies else-where. It is slow in coming, often pressed into the background, forgotten, for years. Its voice cannot be heard in exuberance, nor in battle. It calls us, knocks at our hearts patiently, persis-tently, in what at first is a secret yearning—one can perhaps best describe it as homesickness of the spirit—a longing which makes one finally turn from the world of entities to the no-thing, in an authentic yearning for the Holy.

When does this happen? Not, of course, in an actual decision to surrender, for this is still a deed—terminal, actual, momentary, willed. Repentance like releasement is a state of being, an openness in creative passivity. To hold oneself in surrender occurs only as a gift. It is what has been called above thinking thankfulness. One does not perform acts of repentance, one repents. One *is in* repentance. The gift comes through suffering which, in its pain, opens up the heart to a recognition that all striving is of little value if it does not bring with it a surrender toward gentleness and peace; that power is *truly* powerful only when it is no longer needed; that the Will to Power is weakness.

The Paradox of Existence

There seems to be a strange paradox in human existence: as children we are born in utter helplessness and dependence. This vulnerability holds us open to trustfulness and to a sense of wonder. In hopeful expectancy we view the world around us and our own life. Our "endless" future seems full of joy. Our past, so limited, has little to teach us of disappointment and pain. We are childlike, accepting, trustful, naturally loving. Disappointments and pain, however, invariably mar our course. We learn that the joys of life are not gratuitous, that love is not always returned and is often rejected. The bitterness of life, its loneliness and pain, encounters us in our present, flows into our past and threatens our future. We act and react, we fight, we hurt and are hurt. We are strong, take charge; we are defeated and bow before the inevitable; we are victors and vanquished. We sin, and the exhortation to become childlike once more calls us toward change, *metanoia* — repentance beckons; freedom calls. What we were naturally as children, grew away from in our youth and adulthood, calls to us in our old age. "Unless you become as little children, you shall not enter the kingdom of heaven" (Matt. 18:3).

Repentance, it seems, is the gift of old age (whenever "old age" and its wisdom grace us). It is that gentle recognition that the matters and concerns of "adult" behavior are the concerns —

legitimate as they may have seemed at the time — of flight from serenity toward power, from surrender toward self-assertion, from authentic freedom to inauthentic happiness, from thoughtfulness to thoughtlessness. When this recognition is given to us, a change occurs. This change is often misunderstood by the "adult" world around the aged. It is often viewed as silly: the old *do* things *one* does not do. They seem weak, concerned about such trifles, helpless, childish. We treat them accordingly but, sadly, *not* with the gentleness we show to children. After all, they should know better. In our treatment of them their repentance is enhanced, for they can only be who they are. The more helpless they become, the more they are graced with the surrender of repentance and, paradoxically, the freer they become.

It is, of course, possible for them to reject grace — to become hard and bitter, to retain a cynicism until death. Not every old person is wise, but wisdom comes to us out of the past and, as such, it is the grace of the aged.

Perhaps in these times — times of utility and productivity, of stress and strife, of materialism and atomization, of liberty as action — the repentance concomitant with the surrender of old age is worth a moment of reflection. We are born into this world as children. We depart from it childlike. The return to the wisdom of childlike wonder is a painful process, yet, we are told, it is requisite for the Kingdom of heaven. The Kingdom of heaven, of course, is within. Ours is a "holy place," and in order "to become who we are" we must journey inward in the very act of transcendence.

Our considerations concerning the freedom which is fundamentally ours and is guaranteed us by our Constitution have taken a strange turn. It would seem that, although we are born into democracy, its blessings are ours only through painful effort and that our effort, in fact, consists in surrender to what we are, rather than in frenzied activity directed toward goals external to ourselves.

We are born into life; life with its pain sets us free; authentic freedom in turn brings serenity. The shapers of our Constitution were right: life, liberty, and concomitant happiness are rights basic to the human condition. Could it be, however, that the greatest battle for their survival in democracy has yet to be fought and must, indeed, be fought daily in the heart of each and everyone of us — in the depth of human existence?

3

Toward Solidarity with the Poor

Concern about our calling to be in solidarity with the poor of
this world is widespread among contemporary Christian wom-
en and men. Many of us, over the last several years, having
attended to and reflected upon the writings of liberation theology, now feel an urgency to move from theory to practice, to
effect change — concrete and visible — on behalf of justice. The
number of Christians who (either upon choosing a second ca-
reer or in addition to their first careers) devote themselves in
direct ministry to political and social reform, to work in the
inner city and among the rural poor, has grown significantly.
Social justice task forces, committees, and reflection-action
groups are supported and encouraged by numerous parishes,
religious congregations, youth movements, and ministerial
support groups. Undoubtedly there is movement on behalf of
justice, yet equally clear is evidence of frustration and confusion. The question, What does it *truly* mean to be in *solidarity*
with the poor? seems today, perhaps more so than ever before,
in need of some "depth" probing.

The Paradox of Our Ministries

Ministers who spend their days in heart-rending service, attempting as best they can to heal the wounds of economic
oppression, come home at night exhausted and pained. They

feel the dilemma, the anguish, and perhaps even the guilt that befalls persons who *can* go home and *want* to go home when the day is over (or the month or the year) to a clean bed and bath, to nutritious meals, to recreation and understanding friends, to the occasional shopping spree and movie, a weekend in the mountains, and, generally, enough distance to give them the strength to return and work with renewed effort.

Their anguish springs from their own integrity. It arises from the realization that, given their state in life, true solidarity with the destitute poor will never be theirs.

There are vowed Christians who do not work directly with the poor, who are given to the traditional works of their institutes—education (quite often now in the suburbs), nursing in community-owned medical facilities, keeping community records and finances—but who do feel a frustration similar to the suburban parish priest and minister. This frustration, if not the same as the one described above, nevertheless equals it in intensity. The destitution afflicting the vast majority in this world haunts them also, and they are anguished by impotence and guilt, which many of them feel, even as they try to do what little they can through education, healing, and good stewardship.

What, then, is one to make of this call toward solidarity with the oppressed? What did the Lord mean when he extolled the poor as blessed and promised them the reign of God (Luke 6:20)? Aside from the Christian urgency which compels us all to live simply as Gospel people, sharing with those in need, what more does poverty ask of us? Is authentic solidarity with the poor an impossible option for the educated professional which most of us as ministers are, or is there a deeper, less obvious dimension to poverty which may have escaped us precisely because it is less obvious and lies in the intangible world of the Holy?

Matthew, writing about the same beatitude, claims blessedness for the "poor in *spirit*" (Matt. 5:3). Often, in our concern for the concrete problems of our time, we pass this clarification off too lightly. Yet is it not precisely in the realm of the spirit, in the depth of the self, that solidarity with the poor can be achieved and, indeed, has to be achieved, if we are to be creatively effective in our daily ministries on behalf of justice?

But what do we mean by "the depth of the self," and how can we find there a solidarity with the poor which works of mercy *alone* do not seem to achieve? Besides, maybe the frustration and guilt which we *do* feel is ultimately justified by our "not having done enough" yet, or not having sufficiently identified and then adequately "tackled" the sources of injustice?

Poverty as Disposition

Perhaps the parable of the prodigal son may give us a hint in reflective response to this latter question that must be pondered before we even begin to wonder about the former. I think that what quite frequently seems to escape us in this story is the overemphasis which both sons place on their actions, their concrete behavior. The younger sees his deeds as rendering him undeserving of the Father's forgiveness; the older sees his labor as justifying him. Excessive preoccupation with what they have *done* blocks both of them from authentic at-oneness with their Father and with each other. The younger son does not expect wholehearted forgiveness and is quite prepared to accept the position of servant if only his hunger is alleviated. The older agrees with this assessment and is angry with the Father's totally different value identification. His is an ethics of the head; the Father's is an ethics of the heart. The head justifies logically, according to the laws of cause and effect, crime and punishment. The heart sees beyond reason and celebrates that the son or daughter who "was dead" has returned to life. It is organic: oriented toward healing. Neither the accumulation of vices nor the grand total of virtues is of major importance, for that alone matters which, in the final analysis, leads to tenderness and compassion.

The teachings of Jesus are replete with reminders stressing

works, but rejecting self-justification (or deprecation) by their accumulation. Nor does Jesus encourage an undue emphasis on success. Justification in this parable, as in the parables of the laborers in the vineyard, the pharisee and the publican; as in the calls of Levi, Zacchaeus, the woman at the well, and the adultress, lies in the heart of God. I do not wish to say that works in behalf of justice are unimportant. I simply wish to emphasize that justification does not go by "batting average" or "brownie points." Not even the corporal works of mercy, if considered in themselves as tickets toward a higher rung of glory, will add to my stature as a minister of the Gospel or gift me with authentic solidarity with the oppressed. Is it not noteworthy that Jesus when speaking of their excellence stresses the disposition of those who performed them? "Lord, when did we see you hungry and give you to eat?" they ask (Matt. 25:37), and need to be reminded of the occasion. Their whole life had been immersed in service and had been permeated by that all-encompassing attitude which *is* solidarity without claiming it.

Not long ago a discussion with some colleagues about working "directly with the poor" and sharing this experience with others whose ministries were "not involved in direct service of this kind," caused one of my friends who ministers in the inner city to reject very explicitly yet very simply such classification. "I work with *people*," she said, "I want to be with them, share with them. I do not consider myself different from or more in line with the call to justice than others who do not work where I do. I do not feel comfortable with these distinctions." As important as her *work* is among the economically oppressed in this country, it seemed to me when I heard her say this that her *solidarity* with them sprang from being in touch with a *deeper source*. This deeper dimension, "the depth of the self," as I called it above, is, as I see it, prior to works—not necessarily in time, but essentially *in disposition*. From it wells up all that is good and sacred in human reality.

The reason, I think, why we so frequently ignore it, even as we are busy doing justice, is our excessive dependence on the age-old value structure of what Matthew Fox has so clearly described as "Jacob's Ladder,"[1] and what I like to identify as the religious version of the Will to Power. It has to be recognized for what it is, or it will deny us the solidarity we seek: it will keep us apart from those we serve while under its sway (since they become the recipients of our "works" *for* the Kingdom, not the life-givers whose need is gift to us); as well, it will keep us from those who minister differently, those with whom "Jacob's Ladder" puts us (whether we are conscious of it or not) in continuous competition.

Depth Dimension of Poverty

The depth dimension of the self, on the other hand, is the wellspring of our creative response to the Holy. It refers us to the Kingdom within which, as we will discover and as Jesus tells us, can be the authentic reign of God only when it is grounded not in accumulated works but in our own personally owned and acknowledged "ontological poverty."[2] Quite simply, then, we are in solidarity with the poor only if we ourselves are poor.

At this point it has become necessary to reflect on the meaning of poverty and to identify its scope. Hunger, poverty, vulnerability, weakness are Christian virtues. We are told so in the Magnificat; Christ tells us in the Beatitudes; Paul, in the second letter to the Corinthians. It seems that the Almighty needs our poverty, has made us to be poor so that S/He might "fill the hungry with good things" (Luke 1:53) and have His/Her strength "made perfect in weakness" (2 Cor. 12:9). How are we to understand this and make scriptural passages like these relevant for our lives? It is clear that the term *poverty* as used above exceeds material distinctions. There are the materially poor, the morally poor, those poor in health be it physical or mental, those poor in reputation, in education, in friends. The Lord calls all of these persons blessed and He does so publicly, clearly — to insure, as it were, that they recognize their blessedness and rejoice, lest ignorance might lead them to hanker after the "fleshpots of Egypt" that would enslave them.

The blessedness of the poor, it would seem (that which unites persons in every category mentioned above as well as every other imaginable sense of poverty, and has them stand in solidarity with each other), is their *need* and, even more so, their *knowledge* of their need, for it is *this* that renders them open, receptive, grateful. It is this, in fact, which most authentically gives them their essential dignity as persons (from Latin *per*, "through," and *sonare*, "sound"): those who are open enough and empty enough, in need enough to receive and to give forth (return to the giver) what they have received, through gratitude. A "person" is one *through whom* the sound of creative love can flow, one who can receive and respond in the utter vulnerability of releasement.[3] As such, s/he is blessed in a very basic sense; s/he is poor.

Poverty *as virtue* belongs to all who are authentic persons. Or perhaps more clearly stated: all are poor in direct proportion to their personal integrity and authenticity *as* persons. It may at this point be timely to insist that the above reflection is in no way an attempt at understating the "real" blood-and-guts issue of material poverty: the suffering endured by those deprived of what is rightfully theirs as human beings in a human community. It is merely an attempt to explore and bring to language the experience of poverty in its depth dimension where alone *solidarity* is possible. The poverty explored here is a possibility for all of humankind (rich or poor, healthy or sick, socially acceptable or outcast), because of the simple truth of personhood toward which all are called through the process of maturation, that is, sanctification. By the very fact, of course, that it is a possibility for all, it can also be rejected by anyone — rich and poor alike. Those who are "full of themselves," be they material-

ly advantaged or deprived, will of necessity be "sent away empty." The reign of God cannot be theirs for they experience no
need and therefore cannot receive. As Brennan Manning so
beautifully puts it:

> When we deny our inherent poverty, danger lurks in getting too
> affluently involved with ourselves. Either we begin to make
> demands for things we think we deserve . . . or we blithely take
> for granted everything that comes our way. The poor experience
> genuine gratitude and appreciate the slightest gift. The more we
> grow in the spirit of Jesus Christ, the poorer we become. The
> more we realize that everything is gift [the more] the tenor of
> life becomes one of humble, joyful thanksgiving.[4]

The so frequently heard observation among the materially
advantaged that "poor people are proud" and that one has to be
"careful not to hurt their feelings" when one gives them things,
springs, as I see it, from the Jacob's Ladder mentality mentioned earlier, in which some are seen as "up," others as "down."
Some, then, of necessity have to "look down" on others who
"haven't quite made it" and "reach out a helping hand" to pull
them "up" whenever possible. Charity within this mentality is
hierarchical, dichotomized. It loses its vibrancy, its passion,
and becomes condescension. People are split apart, depersona-
lized, alienated, rather than united. Com-passion — the authentic being-with another in pain — simply has no place. The
world view of Jacob's Ladder sees, as Matthew Fox puts it,
"justice as judgment" (even the *doing of justice* which the Gospel
mandates). It sees "mercy as pity."[5]

Anyone in our age can fall victim to this mentality, for it
pervades our society like a fog and divides us into the camps of
the "deed-oriented" sons of the parable discussed earlier: those
who *deserve* and those who don't; those who *give* and those who
ought to be grateful for anything; those who "make a *decent* living"
and those on welfare; "decent folk" and those "they cannot associate with."

The Virtue of Poverty

The virtue of poverty undercuts this mind-set. In poverty, experienced and owned, lies that authentic solidarity of which I am deprived both when I see another as "poor" without *knowing* the depth of my own want, and when I see another as "rich" and resent what s/he has, despising myself in my want. The virtue of poverty brings me home to my *self* as blessed, as exuberantly happy, because I am in need and know it; I am a sinner and am the beloved of God. The virtue of poverty is *gift* (contrary to anything we may have learned about "virtue" as acquired through repeated efforts on our part). It graces us when we least expect it and, often times, least *deserve it* (if this terminology still creeps into our thoughts). It comes to those who wait, to those who earnestly pray:

> Only prayer reveals the unfathomable depths of our poverty. Submission to it involves an awareness of Someone else. We are so poor that even our poverty is not our own; it belongs to the mysterium tremendum of God. In prayer we drink the dregs of our poverty, professing the plenitude and majesty of Someone else. The ultimate word of the poor in spirit is: "Not I, but Thou." The impoverished man drains the cup when he disappears into the tremendous poverty which is adoration of God (Thomas Merton). "He has learned to stand before God with open hands, not clinging to anything" (Peter Van Breemen).[6]

The virtue of poverty comes as a double-edged sword, a bitter blessing, a *felix culpa* owned: for me, it was the summer of 1982. I had been involved in a bitter struggle for months. Habits which had been mine from youth had brought me to the level of complete intolerance with myself, yet I could not control them. They "had" me and I felt low, broken and very keenly aware of my own weakness and need. At the same time I was struggling with the meaning of *poverty*. I had been to several workshops and discussion groups. I filled the books I was reading with annotations whenever I read even the slightest remark about the issues of justice, oppression, and social responsibility. I felt that much of the talk on the topic was either empty or angry—not helping me to reach any personal depth of my own. Then one night I had a dream: I was led by my twin sister holding me by the hand (as a wisdom figure would) into a room full of women all of whom were severely deformed. They were identified to me as sisters and reached out to me, smiling, and wishing to embrace. Overcoming what I clearly felt as revulsion, I touched and embraced them. One of them offered me some bitter-tasting bread which I ate. Then we left. My guide warned me that eating the bread made me become like them. With this the dream ended. It became clear to me as I reflected on my dream experience during prayer that day that none of the women, including my guide, were strangers or even personalities outside of me. All were dimensions of myself yearning for reconciliation. The bread I had been offered, the bread I had "broken with them," marked our communion. The deformed women longed for solidarity with *me*. Those broken aspects of myself, hidden sources of my shame, were really gifts to me—oh, happy faults—for they exposed me to my brokenness and liberated me from the fleshpots of perfectionism and self-righteousness into the desert of need, into the pain of authentic compassion.

That day I became aware of the depth of grace my life had been. The prisons in our country, the slaughter in Beirut, Auschwitz and Dachau no longer were outside of me. I knew, for the first time beyond the level of platitude, the implications of the observation: there go I but for the grace of God.

The virtue of poverty is a bittersweet gift. It cuts through all defenses and exposes our brokenness even as it readies us for healing.

Brennan Manning in his book, *A Stranger to Self-Hatred*, recounts an experience which may help to illustrate how the above "encounter" can influence behavior in one's daily experiences from then on. He had been visiting Covenant House in New York City, when late one afternoon he walked into the streets:

> I saw a musclebound pimp screaming filth at one of the girls in his stable, I pretended not to notice. Ahead, the movie marquee blinked "kiddie porn" and cautioned the fainthearted not to venture inside. On the corner, two Hispanic hookers in their mid-twenties were soliciting unwary customers. I retreated into a doorway and proceeded to pass through several shades of the emotional spectrum — from a wave of revolt and disgust to anger and frustration and *finally to sadness, emptiness and pain.*[7]

It is this last response, I suggest, which speaks of authentic solidarity with the oppressed. By this I mean of course *all* the oppressed: the hooker, the pimp, the movie theater owner and operator and everyone who ignores what s/he sees as being of no concern to him/her. Undoubtedly, revulsion and disgust, frustration and anger are also part of our response to the injustice permeating our world, but only when we are graced with sadness, with emptiness and with pain, are we in touch with what "is indeed crucial to the evangelical enterprise," namely,

> the awareness that we ourselves are the primary target. It is not "they" who are poor, sinful and lost. It is ourselves. Unless we acknowledge that we are the sinners, the sick ones and the lost sheep for whom Jesus came, we do not belong to the "blessed" who *know* that *they are poor* and inherit the kingdom. . . . Solidarity with human suffering frees the one who receives and liberates the one who gives through the conscious awareness "I am the other."[8]

Nor is there any room for debate here. Once Jacob's Ladder has been undercut by grace, comparative concepts such as higher and lower, worthy and unworthy, noble and ignoble, virtuous and sinful simply cease to make sense. As a dear friend told me once in a moment of pure gift: "I simply can no longer see evil and injustice as 'out there.' I now *know* that there is nothing that I also am not capable of." John Francis Kavanaugh relates this observation very aptly to the Christian community when he says:

> the same behaviors of domination and violence in international, national, and urban groups are potentially operative in a group of men and women who come together to foster and deepen their own Christian lives. If they are able to *face* and purify the patterns of *injustice in their lives together*, they will be able to bring greater compassion as well as *insight* to those patterns which are found at broader social and political levels.[9]

And the insight which is crucially true (never perhaps more so than today when our very integrity as persons and as ministers is at stake in an age where oppression is reaching global consciousness) is the insight that "we are forever passing, back and forth — from 'crucifying the Lord of glory' to being 'nailed to the cross with Christ.'"[10] We can no longer afford to ignore the whole of who we are in favor of partial ideals no matter how apparently sacred they may be, for the whole will claim us. Sooner or later, with a due proportion of pain, it will come home to us that we are light permeated by darkness, truth facing the un-truth within, freedom enslaved, saved and in need of repentance.

Erich Neumann, discussing a new ethic essential for post-Auschwitz humanity, warns us that any "compulsive one-sidedness," be it for the cause of justice, nation, Church, or personal perfection, "is finally overthrown by precisely those elements which it has itself repressed, suppressed or ignored."[11] *Ego inflation*, he warns us, is dangerous not because the value held in high esteem is deficient, but rather because personal or communal limitations are lost sight of. Thus what is valued too highly (in ignorance of the inherent and potential disvalue in all of reality) serves toward dehumanization. The ancients called it *hubris*, and exemplified its disastrous effects in the myth of Icarus: he *had* to fall, for he soared too high. In modern times examples abound. To quote Neumann more extensively:

> The positivist belief in progress was one of the precursors of the First World War, and the arrogation of modern man, regarding himself as the meaning and evolutionary culmination of creation, was a prelude to the bestial arrogation of the Aryan *Herrenvolk* under National Socialism.[12]

Religious zeal and concern for the cause of justice are no exceptions here. There are no "in" theologies, not even liberation theology. There are no "different" spiritualities: one for the rich and one for the poor. There is only one Gospel and one Christ who dies in each of us daily and rises in us even as He calls us toward our own personal and communal integrity. "It is Jesus — not any privileged group, not even any Christian group — who has conquered the world of darkness and death."[13] When we own the radical poverty of our being; when we spend every ounce of our love in the service of justice, yet hold ourselves before God, and find ourselves before our sisters and brothers, empty, receptive, and vulnerable, then we can speak of solidarity with the poor, for then we *are* poor. Then we are truly blest, for the virtue of poverty will have graced us, and we can stand in radical at-oneness with all of humanity in Christ.

Notes

1. Matthew Fox, *A Spirituality Named Compassion and the Healing of the Global Village, Humpty Dumpty and Us* (Minneapolis: Winston Press, 1979), p. 37.

2. John Francis Kavanaugh, *Following Christ in a Consumer Society* (Maryknoll, N.Y.: Orbis Books, 1981), p. 71.

3. See chaps. 1 and 2 for an explanation of this term.

4. Brennan Manning, T.O.R., *The Wisdom of Accepted Tenderness* (Denville, N.J.: Dimension Books, 1978), p. 90.

5. Fox, *A Spirituality Named Compassion*, p. 43.

6. Manning, *Wisdom*, p. 91.

7. Brennan Manning, T.O.R., *A Stranger to Self-Hatred* (Denville, N.J.: Dimension Books, 1982), p. 117 (italics mine).

8. Ibid., pp. 119, 120 (italics mine).

9. Kavanaugh, *Following Christ*, p. 119 (italics mine).

10. Sebastian Moore, *The Crucified Is No Stranger* (London: Darton, Longman & Todd, 1977), p. xi.

11. Erich Neumann, *Depth Psychology and a New Ethic* (New York: Harper Torchbooks, 1973), p. 42.

12. Ibid.

13. Kavanaugh, *Following Christ*, p. 114.

4

Pain: On Letting It Be

Unless the grain of wheat falls to the earth
and dies it remains just a grain of wheat. . . .
If anyone would serve me, let him follow me. . . .
My soul is troubled now, yet what should I
say — Father save me from this hour? But it
was for this that I came to this hour.
(John 12:24–27)

My God, my God, why have you forsaken me?
(Mark 15:34)

Can you drink the cup I shall drink or be
baptized in the same bath of pain as I?
(Mark 10:38)

Blessed . . . are the sorrowing . . .
(Matthew 5:4)

We are all familiar with these passages from Scripture. Their
meaning seems clear enough: that Christ had to die to set us
free. If we are to follow Him, we too will encounter our cross.
We have heard this interpretation on numerous occasions. It is

frequently followed by an explication of suffering that is associated with the injustice of a world that has rejected God, or with our own sinfulness. Christ, it is claimed, was crucified because we are sinners. His own sanctity did not *require* the cross but *accepted* it for us.

True as the above may seem to us in the context of faith, I wonder whether, as we journey ever more deeply into God, an interpretation such as this is sufficient; whether, in other words, "this is all there is" to the Crucifixion and to pain.

The Gospel tells us that we are "blessed" if and when we "sorrow"; that in order to be more than we are (to transcend ourselves) we must "die"; we must be "baptized" in a divine "bath of pain." Is this pain, I wonder, a necessary evil through which we *must pass*, or is it, rather, a requisite which, as the Beatitudes tell us, causes us to be the blessed ones of the Kingdom?

We reflect on the fact that the Holy One had to be utterly forsaken before He could rise. Was this necessary because He was "disfigured" by our sins, or was it *because* He was holy?

This last question may shock us, for it bluntly suggests a relation between holiness and pain. Furthermore, it not only implies that God approves of pain but also that S/He suffers. Our shock at such a suggestion most likely originates in our traditional interpretation of perfection. Suffering, we have hitherto been taught, arises out of a lack, an incompleteness. How, then, can the Perfect One suffer? To jolt us further is the other question that flows logically out of this tradition and was answerable only by an association of pain with sin, namely: How can the Holy One allow those S/He loves to suffer?

Unless pain is associated with sin, and the latter (being a free act) attributed to humankind, God will appear to have willed it. Within the contemporary Western cult of pleasure (which seems to have permeated all thought, even our theologies), this would be tantamount to accusing God of willing evil.

Is Pain Evil?

But is pain evil? If, for the sake of our reflection, we would, at least tentatively, take the "revolutionary" view that it need not be, all sorts of possibilities might open up for us. First, perfection and pain would no longer be irreconcilable and one could then reflect upon a suffering God. Furthermore, our own pain would no longer necessarily be punishment for our freely chosen evil acts or those of others; nor would it have to be the unhappy by-product of an imperfect universe. Although these possibilities need not be denied, pain could then find a place on a deeper level, namely, *within* holiness as such.

I have always been uncomfortable with the uncompromising teachings of Christians who minister as healers through prayer alone. Sickness, many of them claim, is not the will of God and, somehow, only the result of our inability to channel divine healing energies. Jesus cured all those who came to Him in faith. He does not want us to suffer.[1] When I read such theories, I always want to object that this approach seems to me too simple and, somehow, impoverishing. It occurs to me that the very finite embodiment of the Son of God made it impossible for Him to cure all those who came for healing. It could be argued that by assuming finitude for His mission He assented, at least indirectly, to suffering: the pain of those He could not reach because of His own limitations, and the pain for Himself in the knowledge of this.

Jesus called those who sorrow "blessed" while, at the same time, He busied Himself in healing many of their afflictions. He assumed the cross — was "bathed" in pain, yet He too, in the garden, prayed to be delivered "from this hour." Nevertheless, He challenged others to take up their cross as He had done, to assume pain as a "sign" of holiness ("if you will be perfect"), and to die in order to bring about personal transformation. If one were to argue that those who sorrow are "blessed" *because* they will be comforted and thus restored to a state without sorrow, then one would have to ask why those who do not require this restoration are not blessed also, and if so, why Jesus took the trouble of making this puzzling statement in the first place. One is left to wonder whether, perhaps, a dynamic between the *sorrow* and the *comforting* (pain entered in upon, held within oneself, acknowledged, embraced without fear) makes for the blessedness.

Christ's repeated exhortation while among us was "fear not." Might He have come primarily to liberate us from *fear* rather than from pain? If this were so, one would have to distinguish between two dispositions toward pain integrally related to holiness and Christ's saving mission: (1) the *flight* from pain characterized by denial, anger, projection, self-hate, and hatred of others as well as of the Other. All these are essentially related to the fear from which Christ came to free us. (2) An *acceptance* of pain (to be differentiated from a morose search *for* pain and suffering) which enters, as it were, "into the eye of the storm," holds itself there and is held there by a strength which can only be ascribed to grace: "for they shall be comforted."

Pain and the Holy One

Reflection upon the paradox of pain leads me to the suggestion that God not only is capable of suffering but that, in fact, pain is *of God*, and a refusal of pain, an aspect of the *human*, all-too-human, condition. Pain, I propose, can be holy, not only in its consequences (God drawing good out of evil) but also in its nature. The "perfection" of humanness is the embracing of *holy* pain, not for the sake of anything other but, in fact, for the sake of pain itself as the breakthrough of God in us.

To explain further, there is no doubt, I think, that human beings whom we call great are great because of their encounter with pain. Psychologists tell us, and often personal experience does so as well, that the sensitive person—the one most "in touch" with his/her humanness—is also the one most in pain: what the dull ear cannot hear, the composer picks up in anguish or rejoicing; what the dull heart cannot feel, the lover endures with passion. Love, for that matter, is the example par excellence of ecstatic pain. The lover virtually stands outside him/herself in a yearning for wholeness with the other. This, however, is brought about only, it seems, in the very acknowledgment of the pain. When I say yes to my longing, the other is brought near, as it were, to my heart, for I acknowledge my need of him/her and recognize in anguish what I might otherwise have taken for granted. Only the *vulnerable* can truly experience love. For those sufficient unto themselves, love remains empty.

It continues to be a puzzle to me why we can so freely ascribe pain to the highly sensitive spirit, ecstatic passion to the lover, yet refuse it to God. Concerning this, the Russian philosopher Berdyaev shares a superb reflection:

> It is extraordinary how limited is the human conception of God. Men are afraid to ascribe to Him inner conflict and tragedy characteristic of all life, the longing for His "other," for the birth of man, but have no hesitation in ascribing to Him anger, jealousy, vengeance and other affective states which, in man, are regarded as reprehensible.[2]

Berdyaev sees an amazing contradiction between our view of personal perfection and our interpretation of divine perfection. God, we declare, is self-sufficient, immobile, tyrannical almost: demanding uncompromising submission. These attributes, however, we consider despicable when applied to humans.

> People are afraid to ascribe movement to God, because movement indicates the lack of something, or the need for something

that is not there. But it may equally well be said that immobility is an imperfection, for it implies the lack of the dynamic quality of life.[3]

Berdyaev sees "tragic conflict" in God as a sign of perfection. The God and Creator of life possesses the attributes of life holistically. S/He is dynamic not immobile, flowing out in Self-gift and yearning for all things to return to Him/Her. God is revealed in our Christian tradition as "sacrificial love" which, "far from suggesting self-sufficiency implies the need of passing into its 'other.'"[4] Sacrifice implies tragedy and tragedy implies pain. If the Christian God is a God of sacrificial love (a truth no believer can deny), then pain — the birth-pain which opens to fullness of life — is Creator-pain. Nature — the handiwork of God — is filled with pain; its dying for the sake of life is a continuous rhythm, "cruel" no doubt, to the thoughtless observer who, by projecting upon the flow of life his/her own inability or unwillingness to embrace creative pain, remains empty in his/her escape.

A self-sufficient deity cannot create out of love, for love longs for union which self-sufficiency contradicts. A union denied because of freedom demands that love assume freedom in order to open the way of return. Christ-love is sacrificial love which embodies the death-pain of this return. "Unless the grain of wheat falls to the earth and dies it remains *just a grain of wheat*" (John 12:24).

I have reflected on the possibility that the dynamic perfection of God holds the pain of tragedy within it. This would imply, as I have already mentioned, not only that God is capable of pain but also that pain is integrally of God as Creator and Savior. God, as it were, flows out in longing for the free other and, because this freedom has rejected Him/Her, breaks through into freedom: takes on its form and becomes the *Way* in pain and sacrificial love.

Pain and Human Maturation

Human love, it seems, is called to do likewise: to be "baptized in the same bath of pain," to continue the Good News and respond to the divine yearning by its own longing for its source. Human pain is homesickness for the beginning. The death we are called to endure is the death *to* separation and *toward* wholeness. The human condition is the story of this life-oriented dying. It is the Gospel individualized. It is the Christ-story in each of us.

Much has been written, especially in contemporary times, about the maturing process. Today, in particular, interest is beginning to focus on mid-life. The "mid-life crisis" has been accepted as a fact. The word *crisis*, of course, implies pain; somehow it is hoped that by writing about it, explaining it, dealing with it, one can help people through it with a bit less struggle.

Noble as these intentions may be, I wonder whether helping the person to move *into* it rather than *through* it would not, in the last analysis, prove more beneficial. Pain, I repeat, is too often viewed as something to be avoided or at most discarded quickly, rather than as grace to be embraced.

Bernard J. Boelen describes the mid-life crisis as the "crisis of the limits."[5] It is, as the word suggests, the pain of the *turning point* from an action-oriented existence — dominated by the concern for establishing oneself, for succeeding in life, for *doing* — to a Being-oriented existence, where one's vocation is no longer found in *what one achieves* but in *who one is*. Boelen suggests that the ultimate yes to one's limits is requisite for opening the door to *maturity as a way* — never an accomplished fact, but ever an ongoing process. That the yes is acknowledged as pain-filled is evident, as was already suggested, in the use of the word *crisis*. Boelen, in fact, maintains that the lifelong flowering into wholeness which is maturation is a continuous dying directed

toward deeper life, a passing from one existential crisis to another—into greater openness.

Crises, then, are not extraordinary events, occurring in the
person because of a mishap in the external circumstances of
his/her life. They are part of the totality of his/her dynamic
openness to Being. The pain implied by existential crises,
therefore, is a pain inherent in the creation process. It is the
same pain as the one we have above ascribed to God.

Such pain is creative, for its yearning is to flow back into
God who is its beginning and its end. As such, the recognition
and acceptance of one's limits in achievement is an anguish
which opens the heart to surrender and to the yearning for
union which, in the agony of its longing, is already coming
about.

Such pain is redemptive, for the pain of acknowledging one's
limits opens the person to freedom: a freedom deeper than the
limits; a freedom that speaks of surrender, of an obedience (a
listening) to one's being, of releasement born of repentance.

In acknowledging our limits we take up the cross of our own
poverty; we become childlike; we let (in Jungian terminology)
the ego surrender to the self and, in Sebastian Moore's interpretation of this, the crucifier embrace the crucified.[6] Each of
us says, "I want to come home," and in stillness and in pain
knows that his/her home is in the journey. Holiness as maturity
is a dynamic process. In sacrificial love we *are* holiness on the
way.

Pain and Daily Life

What application has this discussion about pain to our daily
lives? What is it that one should *do* about pain? Should one
ignore the suffering in the world and simply abide in one's own
recognition that ultimately pain is holy? Would that the answer
were simple!

To begin with, suffering inflicted through injustice cannot be ignored. An unjust act is evil, and if it is within our power to put a halt to injustice, our integrity calls us to do this. This does not of course deny that pain endured by the oppressed *can* hold the holy within it (as was indeed the case with Christ crucified), but ours is hardly the role of judging what pain is or is not good for another. As far as our being-together-with-others is concerned, we are called to works of mercy even as Jesus was. We are not commanded to seek pain for ourselves or endure pain that could be alleviated. Masochism is an illness, not a virtue.

All this is not disputed by what I have said in this chapter. My concern here is simply with the pain inherent in life and in the life process. Life and vibrant holiness are pervaded with pain; pain, as such, is of the holy and, if embraced, sanctifies. I contend that our own limitations (painful to us, without a doubt) carry within them the cut-off points for alleviating the pain of others. As the mystery of pain unfolds in our lives and in the lives of those we love, we often find ourselves suffering with the other whom we cannot help. At such times, we must trust that pain is holy. Pain as *holy* is of the whole, as Heidegger would have us see:

> Pain rends. It is the rift. But it does not tear apart into dispersive fragments. Pain indeed tears asunder, it separates, yet so that at the same time it draws everything to itself, gathers it to itself. Its rending as a separating that gathers, is at the same time that drawing which, like the pen drawing of a plan or sketch, draws and joins together what is held apart in separation. Pain is the *joining agent in the rending that divides* and *gathers*.[7]

In rending the heart, pain holds our love as one in the Holy. Through it we take part in the dynamic flow of life and learn com-passion, the "perfection" of God.[8] In our poverty we must trust that suffering leads the other, in ways we do not know, toward inwardness and wholeness. By surrendering ourselves to the pain of our incapacity to alleviate suffering we learn to let pain *be*. We say yes to its salvific/creative dimension. Thus we release ourselves to the breakthrough of God in our lives.

Notes

1. See A. Sanford, *The Healing Light* (Plainfield, N.J.: Logos International, 1976). Although I agree with much of Agnes Sanford's work, her almost radical denial of the goodness of suffering puzzles me.

2. Nicolas Berdyaev, *The Destiny of Man* (New York: Harper Torchbooks, 1960), p. 28.

3. Ibid.

4. Ibid.

5. Bernard J. Boelen, *Personal Maturity* (New York: Seabury Press, 1978), chap. 6.

6. Sebastian Moore, *The Crucified Is No Stranger* (London: Darton, Longman & Todd, 1977), pp. ix–xii.

7. Martin Heidegger, *Poetry, Language, Thought*, trans. Albert Hofstadter (New York: Harper & Row, 1971), p. 204 (italics mine).

8. Matthew Fox, *A Spirituality Named Compassion and the Healing of the Global Village, Humpty Dumpty and Us* (Minneapolis: Winston Press, 1979), p. 10.

5

Obedience Reconsidered

As Christian men and women we find ourselves today, more than ever before, radically immersed in a wounded and broken world. The contemplative mode of embracing the realities of our time, which the Gospel demands of all those who would authentically follow Jesus, challenges us, therefore, toward an equally radical reexamination of our mission in accordance with the evangelical counsels to which we are committed by our baptism and, some of us, by vows.

Much has been and is being written these days about our calling to express solidarity with the poor; in this regard, we are especially grateful to our brothers and sisters expressing a theology of liberation. Celibacy and chastity too are being rethought in the light of a more truly relational mode of living toward which vowed religious and Christians generally are evolving. Our consciousness on these matters has been raised particularly by the psycho-theology arising from a deeper understanding of Jung and other contemporary humanistic psychologists (such as Frankl, May, Maslow, and Rogers, as well as others). What seems, however, to remain unresolved for many of us today is the question concerning the place of evangelical obedience in the vowed as well as the broader Christian life of our times.[1]

Today's emphasis on individuality as an essential dimension of community has led us to place a more authentic stress on inwardness and personal responsibility. It calls us to listen with greater intensity than ever before to the fundamental questions (which Sebastian Moore has identified as, in a sense, prereligious but also, and ultimately, mystical questions[2]) of human existence: "who am I?" "Why am I?" Thus discernment has become personalized. Shakespeare's advice, "To thine own self be true," is, as it were, receiving unquestioning support. Many men and women among us, however, are beginning to wonder whether the communal dimension represented by the second part of this exhortation, "thou canst not then be false to any man,"[3] is considered with equal enthusiasm especially when, upon reflection, its implications are brought home to us.

While concern for personal fulfillment is undoubtedly essential for the authentic development of the whole community, it is precisely this latter objective which presents us now with some unsettling questions. Perhaps the words of Victor Frankl, though they were expressed within the context of psychotherapy several years ago, are nevertheless still best suited for placing the issue into perspective. In a lecture dealing with "The Philosphical Foundations of Logotherapy" he stresses the necessity for the transcendent dimension of inwardness, or what might also be interpreted as the communal dimension of individual authenticity (our essential being as *cobeing*): "self-actualization, like power [Adler] and pleasure [Freud], also belongs to the class of phenomena which can only be obtained as a side effect and are thwarted precisely to the degree to which they are made a matter of direct intention."[4] Criticizing other psychotherapeutic theories as inadequate because of their excessive stress on the individual, he emphasizes that the person is "a being *encountering other beings* and reaching out for meanings to fulfill" *through* this encounter.[5]

The unsettling questions facing us today, as we live more deeply into the meaning of community, are precisely those questions which hold us in the tension between our individual quests and our communal and global obligations. The issue, therefore, revolves around what might be called a crisis of obedience. By this I do not mean that Christians are no longer heeding authority nor that a general chaos—the usual result of everyone doing his/her "own thing"—has taken over our communities. The crisis (a turning point) is much deeper, more fundamental than this. Its basic question is at the roots of evangelical commitment and asks "into" the meaning of obedience *as such*, wondering how authority today can be authentic.

Etymologically, *obedience* implies *listening* (Latin *obedire*, "to listen to"). Listening, it would seem, springs from a desire to receive a response, and a response is the logical consequence of a question asked. This was indeed until very recently (and may still be for some of us) the sequence of obedience and authority as we experienced it. Somehow we saw authority vested with the answers for our obedient compliance. The question asked (if not explicitly, then implicitly) by our very presence in a communal context concerned the *how* of faithfulness to the Church, that is, the Christian community generally and the familial or vowed life in particular. The answer came from beyond us and through appointed authority. I do not wish to deny the validity of this position under certain circumstances, for holiness was undoubtedly wrought through listening surrender within the above scheme of things. I also do not wish to insinuate that this interpretation of obedience is now completely absent from our everyday transactions, from the way we understand ourselves in relation to others in our community. The feelings of insecurity and discomfort which so frequently befall us when we are presented with dilemmas, with questions which demand an answer but seemingly have none; the temptations we then feel to shelve the question, to move on in the agenda, to dismiss the person expressing the question, to distract ourselves from standing in the tension of the unsolvable, all point to the fact that consciously or not we are still held captive by the sequence of obedience and authority described above—a sequence which is rational, orderly, and as such seems fitting for a world planned by an all wise God as we "understand" Him/Her.

I intend neither to reject this concept of obedience totally nor to suggest that it no longer is held by us, at least in some form. Rather, I wish to invite the reader to probe more deeply into the meaning of this virtue in order to see whether, in another dimension, on what may be a more fundamental level, new insights may be possible; whether they are, in fact, already emerging and may indeed be necessary for our times.

Foundational Obedience

What if the *listening* constituted by foundational obedience were not a waiting for an answer, but for a question? What if the question which would give itself to the waiting heart were such that an adequate response could only be a deeper question? What if the meaning of authority within the context of obedience just described were understood etymologically as "authoring" (Latin *augere*), as giving increase, building, edifying?[6] Would not the concept of leadership in our communities then *have* to undergo a radical crisis, come to a turning point, which would shift it from the role of supplying answers to that of authoring questions? Would not leadership then, above all, consist in an attentive openness to the signs of our time, a passionate waiting (with all the pain that this implies) for the questions which radically address us in our age? Would not the waiting which constitutes this leadership be, indeed, what the root of the word silently beckons us to understand, namely, a surrender in *service* to the truth which reveals itself as enigmatic? An old wisdom figure in my life, Fritz Heidegger (brother of the famous philosopher) shared this with me shortly before he died:

> The most important dimension of authentic
> living is patience.
> It shows itself in the smallest, most
> insignificant events.

> Greatness of spirit manifests itself
> in one's capacity to wait.
> Patience is strength as well as great
> pain.
> The being of love is found in patience.

Standing in service to the truth in patient waiting for its self-disclosure as mystery: Would not this understanding of authority identify it in the most radical sense with obedience?

The crisis of obedience, as I see it today, is the crisis of an existential shift (conscious or unconscious) from the former experience which somehow is still with us, to a new, not yet articulated experience concomitant with our age. Questions no longer have simple, and in many cases not even complicated, answers. We live, as I mentioned already, in a broken world and, in our radical union with this world, are ourselves broken. Our Christian mission, if it is to be healing both for ourselves and others, must come to grips with its own wounds. The questions which present themselves cannot be answered glibly but must be "lived into" with passionate endurance and waiting. As Heidegger reminds us in his *Letter on Humanism*: to wait means to listen, to be vulnerable, to be poor as a shepherd is poor.[7] Living "into" the question is experiencing the answer in its depth dimension: as a deeper question which does not own the truth as "clear and distinct," but shepherds the mystery.

All this may sound discouraging. We are, after all, children of the age of technology — the age where science promises to leave no problems unsolved, no questions unanswered (provided, of course, they are properly formulated and defined). Whether we are Christians or not, the culture of the twentieth century is part of our heritage. It has left little room for mystery. Truth, even in theology, is seen as light. That this phenomenon is completely meaningless without darkness is a fact that has eluded us for centuries. Only the mystics and some lonely thinkers of our time[8] remind us of the importance of the unfathomable. It is difficult, therefore, to stand in the pain of a question without demanding a resolution. It is difficult, even more so, to face the issues of our time and to wait in humility for the proper questions wherewith to address them. Here is, however, where I see fundamental obedience as the unifying force whereby the evangelical counsels can be affirmed, truly lived today, and whereby holistic—mature—community can happen.

How can we possibly know *poverty* as "solidarity with the poor," for example, unless we can *wait* in reverence and in pain for the revelation of that poverty which permeates our very beings: a poverty which opens us up to humble listening and serving and prevents us from engaging in works of pity instead of mercy.⁹ How can we live relationally as celibates or within the permanent commitment of marriage and, therefore, counterculturally, unless we can allow ourselves to face the uncomfortable questions concerning our own inner darkness; unless we can face the mysteries of the contra-sexual tendencies present in each one of us (Jung's *animus* and *anima* archetypes) and admit to our ever ready willingness to project these upon those whom we encounter? Finding the truth concerning our inner selves as cobeings means living the questions toward the deeper insight of further questions encountered in our reflective being together with others.

As I suggested above, not only the evangelical counsels as such are in dire need of fundamental obedience but also our general communal involvement and our response to the realities facing us as a group, as a family. Questions satisfied by answers and, therefore, brought to closure are by definition static. Dynamic maturity only occurs when we remain on the journey, prophetic, in search for deeper questions. Here alone do we encounter the open-ended, the evolutionary, the growth-filled, the call to be Gospel people.

Today the Christian family, parish, and religious congregation are faced with many questions. Few were ever anticipated. For the most part, they "overtook us" and now require our reflection. Thus, in vowed communities, for example, the lack of vocations almost struck like fate in the night. We were building huge formation houses only to find them half empty within a few years after their construction. Religious communities in many cases are dying, yet there seems such an urgent need for the witness which the Gospel stance of the vowed life can give. Sacramental relationship and permanence of commitment within marriage is today threatened on every side. Loneliness in family and community is epidemic. Do we know the meaning of death? Can we live into the question of the new life which this death might bring? Do we understand the value of the countercultural and can we live into the question which a different lifestyle, demanded of us in this time of destitution, may pose for us? Can we in this nuclear age endure the painful questions of personal atomization, and can we *face* each other *as a community* with these questions — "giving increase," edification, support, understanding? Can we, in other words, *be* the authority that authors new questions and deeper insights through foundational obedience? Can we endure the pain of the misunderstanding which this may bring? Can we point toward authentic values without offering final solutions? Can we be prophets? Prophets are those who live in tension between the world that cries for instant solutions and the God of mystery; who accept the passion of creative waiting and embrace the reign of God as "among us but not yet." They experience in their very being the questioning-response to the call homeward, God-ward. They are the living symbols (from Greek *sun*, "together," and *ballein*, "to throw"[10]), the loci where questions and deeper questions meet and are held together in faith-filled action.

These are difficult questions. They demand the self-emptying asked of discipleship.[11] They demand radical faith, unwavering hope, and courageous love. They are the questions urging us to stand in the turning point of obedience and to author a new vision.

These questions arise in a listening heart and, if heeded, will lead us into our own death and resurrection. They are questions which, I maintain, cannot be avoided and must be taken up by Christian men and women of every type of community, so that authority might authentically reside in the membership of Christ's Body, and we might experience our common priesthood in Christ.

Notes

1. Certainly we cannot overlook such excellent reflections as Dorothee Soelle's *Beyond Mere Obedience*. As the title of her work suggests, she hopes to move beyond what obedience has come to mean and to invite the Christian community to self-fulfillment and creative fantasy. Whereas I wholeheartedly accept her observations concerning the deterioration which our understanding of "obedience" has suffered, I hesitate to abandon or replace the word. Returning to a deeper more radical meaning of obedience seems to me a more authentic encounter with language as "the house of Being" (Heidegger). It seems to me a useless enterprise to eliminate a word which has exercised as significant an influence on Christian living as has obedience. If, as Soelle suggests, people's lives have virtually been "absorbed" by obedience—in most cases to the detriment of their personal development and that of the community—then we are dealing here with more than a mere concept. Obedience elicits a disposition, a fundamental way of being. As such it must be addressed and rethought rather than eliminated from our vocabulary.

2. Sebastian Moore, *The Fire and the Rose Are One* (London: Darton, Longman & Todd, 1980), pp. 12–16.

3. *Hamlet*, act 1, scene 3.

4. Victor Frankl, *Psychotherapy and Existentialism* (New York: Washington Square Press, 1967), p. 8.

5. Ibid.

6. Bernard J. Boelen, *Personal Maturity* (New York: Seabury Press, 1978), p. 158.

7. Martin Heidegger, *Platons Lehre von der Wahrheit mit einem Brief über den Humanismus*, 2nd ed. (Bern: Francke Verlag, 1954), p. 90.

8. I make reference here to Martin Heidegger who sees truth as "un-truth" not in the sense of contradiction, but rather in the sense of mystery, that is, as never fully revealed, as always somewhat withheld. This fact he attributes primarily to the finitude of the truth process taking place in the human person. Heidegger is not alone in this understanding. The theories of quantum physics of Heisenberg and Bohr show physical reality today as *essentially* mysterious also. (See Fritjof Capra, *Turning Point* [New York: Simon and Schuster, 1982], pp. 79, 80.)

9. See chap. 3 of this book.

10. Boelen, *Personal Maturity*, p. 66.

11. Phil. 2:5–11.

6

Toward a Feminine Spirituality

At this point, the thoughtful reader may be experiencing a certain difficulty or frustration in the face of the ministerial disposition which I have been attempting to describe. Such frustration might easily arise out of the cultural bias, the historical frame into which we were born and in which we have been immersed throughout our years of development and education. Releasement (being freed and setting free), poverty as virtue, pain as blessed, obedience as standing in the question toward deeper mystery are not the usual concepts of spirituality with which many of us address the reality of our ministerial lives. Most of us have been raised within what could easily be described as a schizophrenic world view, where clear and distinct ideas direct our behavior and where what is measurable, ascertainable, and demonstrable is valued; anything different from this ("less than this" as many would phrase it) is called into question. Activities which do not yield measurable results seem useless and unpractical. What then is one to do with reflections that stress a disposition of surrender to depth, to involvement with mystery; that identify passion as primary to action, the latter as essentially flowing from the former? This whole attempt might appear nebulous to anyone raised in, and ministering in, an age demanding clarity, precision, verification, and results.

Though this dis-ease might be normal for most of us, I have found it interesting, nevertheless, that over the past few years when I have taught these ideas to graduate students in various programs of ministerial education, it has never yet failed that, along with the puzzlement mentioned above, a certain nostalgia has been evoked, a gentle "aha" experience, if you will, as if something "clicked," fell into place — something long forgotten, or ignored, or perhaps not yet encountered but sought after. I think that the puzzlement or discomfort which the reflections of this book may evoke in us arises not because the ideas are foreign to us, but rather because they do not fit within the paradigm of dualism out of which we are accustomed to function. For the dualistic mind what is different is seen as contradictory and irreconcilable: what is weak can never be strong; what is dark can never be light; what is bad never good; what is female never male. That much of reality gives itself to us in pairs of polar opposites and needs to be held into consciousness as a polar tension of dynamic energy is unacceptable to the dualistic interpreter of reality. Nothing short, therefore, of a conversion or "revolution of consciousness," as Beatrice Bruteau calls it,[1] can move us beyond our estrangement from mystery into the depth dimension of who we are.

It is for this reason that I would like to invite reflection, at this point, about a *feminine* turn in spirituality. I suggest this not to establish a counter position to what has come to be known as a typically masculine form of spirituality and theology, but rather to explore the possibility of identifying the tensions necessary for a creative encounter of those polarities which constitute the reality of our cobeing here on earth and before God.

Why a Feminine Spirituality?

In many fields of leadership today, whether theological, general academic, or even political, much is being discussed about the rights of women. "Women should be listened to and taken seriously" is proclaimed from pulpits, political and academic platforms, and in the media. Yet it is my impression that few if any of the proclaimers ever take the time to seriously investigate *why* this is so. The reason for this "should" seems to be taken for granted. It is regarded as obvious: women's ways of perceiving reality have been reduced to a minority status for centuries. Oppressed groups (and women most definitely are oppressed) *should* be allowed to speak. By identifying these "shoulds," none of which can be denied, the reasons for moving toward the liberation of women have been subsumed under the heading of "doing justice." Yet worthy as this cause may be, somehow when I reflect on all this I am not satisfied, for I cannot help wondering whether anyone has really thought through *what* has been oppressed with respect to women. It must be stressed that I am not talking about the blatant, the obvious signs of oppression: women could not hold public office until recently; they still cannot do so in many churches; they could not vote for a long time and were generally "kept in place." (I do not say *"their* place." It seems to me that no one really knows what "their" place was or even what it is today.) It is clear that out of a sense of social justice liberation is mandatory. But what *precisely* will happen with this liberation? How *will* the feminine affect humankind *once it is allowed to speak*? Why is it paramount that the feminine emerge; paramount both for women and for men? Once again, it seems so easy to address all of these questions merely in terms of social justice or constitutional rights — and I certainly do not wish to deny the importance of equal wages and job opportunities. Yet somehow I sense that freedom fought from within these parameters quickly loses its juice, for here as before men will be giving women their rights. It is men who will invite women to serve on committees; men who will give women equal pay; men who will allow women to wear slacks, play football, do sportscasting, teach in seminaries, become ordained; as a result, somehow, the impression is quickly given that the issue has been solved.

The issue, however, will remain; discontent and anger will

persist, because all that will have been accomplished is that women will have been given, and will have fought for, stereotypical masculine rights but will have been ignored *as* women, that is, in their *feminine dimension*. They will have been allowed into the male world, but its *essential reality* will not have changed. It is true that it will have shrunk: men will have less space, fewer jobs. They will have shared the pie. This undoubtedly will have meant sacrifice and hurt, as doing justice almost always hurts. But the question which remains is whether there will have been transformation. Will there have been *intrinsic* change either in men or in women?

Not long ago a major religious community of men invited me to explore with them the possibility of inviting women to join their formation team. I asked them one simple question: Would they be willing to yield at least twenty-five percent of their formational policies to the insights and perspectives of the women they would be asking to join them. I had made my point. The women were not hired.

Movement Toward a Feminine Spirituality

To hear the fourth Beatitude bless those who hunger and thirst for "holiness" instead of "justice" has always had a more authentic ring for me. Giving another "his/her due," the "doing" of justice, can be quite dry and irritating. To hunger for holiness, on the other hand, transforms, heals, makes whole, for this is what "holiness" means. The movement addressed in this reflection speaks to this issue. Moving toward a feminine perspective on reality is necessary *not* primarily because it is mandated by common decency and justice, but rather because it is inherent in our call to wholeness, to holiness, to completion, to transformation. I propose, therefore, that to be holy men need women and women need men.

Of course holiness, as may be obvious by now, is not something acquired by prescribed actions. I am not concerned, therefore, with the reversal of intermingling of roles, valuable and proper though this may be at times. I am concerned, rather, with an ability to *see*, to share and to value differing perspectives in a common quest for the mystery which cannot be possessed or systematized by anyone. When women in our churches and in the public arena generally will be allowed to *do* what men alone have been doing for centuries, justice will have been served, without doubt. Depth perception, mutuality and wholeness, however, arise on another plane. Sociologically, of course, it can be argued that what people do and are allowed to do is directly proportionate to the way they see themselves and are seen in their relation to others. I do not deny this interconnectedness but wish to stress a more primary conversion of perception without which women will simply adopt a pseudo-masculinity — adopt, if you will, a masculine way of perceiving reality without ever learning to appreciate the treasures hidden within their own uniquely feminine way of being-in-the-world.

An example may help to clarify this issue. A few years ago the women religious of the community to which I belong, in an attempt to acquaint themselves with current theology, invited a well-known speaker and writer to talk on the concept of "local Church." He focused on the idea of broadening the base of leadership within an ecclesial hierarchy. As his symbol he chose to discuss the dialectic between what he called the "downward movement" and the "upward flow." Authority, he claimed, has been presented to us in times past as moving from the top down. The concept of the local Church, however, allows us now to see the validity of moving from the base up. He seemed to feel very good about his symbol as he pointed out to us that, in a sense, it should speak particularly well to us *as women*, since in many ways this opened the road of authority for us also and could be viewed as our feminine alternative. However, his symbol left most of us rather untouched.

Had he been able to widen his perception beyond the perspective of a dominant group; had he, in fact, simply been able to contextualize it a bit more broadly within the history of Western thought, including mysticism, he would have stumbled upon Heraclitus who warns us that the "way up and the way down are one and the same,"[2] or, in later times, Heidegger who observed that every movement against is contained *within* that against which it moves.[3] The hierarchical movement is not challenged by a stress on "upward mobility." Most of us are sadly aware that the oppressed can easily become the oppressor when s/he reaches the top. For a pope or primate *merely* to recognize that pastors have opinions, and for the latter to delegate *some* authority to the laity; for men *finally* to take women seriously is *not* the *feminine alternative* to the dominant modes of cobeing in this world. It may be an example of doing justice, but it is not an example of being whole and embracing the Holy.

But what of the feminine approach? Perhaps another example will make the discussion easier. A friend of mine not long ago shared with me her hope of working out a master's degree project on the spirituality of women. Being an academic by training, I readily asked her the "appropriate" questions: What were her plans? Had she started her research already? Whom would she seek out as advisor? Her response delighted me. Without a single trace of embarrassment about her "nonacademic" style she informed me that together with another student she was hoping to gather together groups of women and move toward a shared exploration of our experience.

What we see in this very simple example is what could be called the phenomenon of *power emerging in the group through mutual empowerment*. Women gathered together coauthor a vision. As we have discussed already, the etymology of the word *authority* leads us to "empowerment," to "giving increase," to affirming another in his/her being. When authority resides in the group there is no need for either sanction or control from without; there is no need to "climb up"; there is no "up"; there is no "down."

Obedience in such a context becomes what we have in our previous reflection identified as a "standing in the question": developing a disposition of openness; being sufficiently empty of preconceptions, stereotypes, jargon, and opinions to genuinely *wait* for the Bridegroom to appear in our midst. Waiting, truly understood, means serving the truth of who we are. It means coming home to vulnerability.

This, I suggest, is the beginning of a new theological method: the deemphasis on closure and on truth addressing us from outside ourselves; the acceptance of unconcealing concealment, as Heidegger would say: of light emerging out of darkness and intermingled with it leaving whatever appears always still partially hidden or mysterious and, therefore, never absolutely clear; of strength out of weakness; of healing out of brokenness; of God within humankind. It is of course not the only method, nor is it totally original. It is *new* only because it has so long been neglected, ignored, and deprecated. This method does not crave the *nihil obstat*, nor does it need official substantiation through citing "authorities" in the field: the "springing from one quotation to the next," as Dorothee Soelle describes it, "without having the courage to use personal talk; the almost anal obsession with footnotes called 'scientific style'; the conscious, but much worse, the unconscious craving for orthodoxy and the shelter it offers to the professional theologian."[4] This method does not need to convince, nor does it need to bring "into the fold."

The reason why the need for official orthodoxy does not arise in this dynamic of obedient coauthoring is not because of rebellion or some sense or overagainstness, nor is it due to a lack of respect for one's heritage and tradition. Its justification lies in its commitment to truth as *emerging* from *within*. One does not receive the truth, nor does one give it. One stands *in* the truth as experience, as it emerges, and one surrenders to that wherein one is held.

When Heidegger tells us that "language is the house of Being," what he means is precisely this: authentic speech as the vehicle of truth *is* the articulation of *who we are*. In dialogue we discover our being. Meaning emerges out of our being-together-with-others in reverence. It is not a functional or a formative tool imposed from the outside. It is the lighting up of an event.

Not long ago the issue of women's liberation came up in a discussion with some colleagues of mine. A confrere suggested that the "truth," as North American women see it, simply does not apply, nor can it be *imposed* upon, women in Africa or elsewhere in the world. He maintained that we would oppress other women by suggesting *liberation* to them because it has not as yet arisen as an issue or a need for them and should therefore not be "pushed on them."

Of course, as we have just said, externally imposed "truth" is oppressive. It has certainly proved oppressive to women for centuries. One simply does not (ought not) force one's view of things on others. One does not *mandate* one solitary interpretation of anything (be it God, human nature, or reality generally) for everyone, with total disregard for difference in culture, in gender, in history. This would not only be oppressive but also unrealistic and unworkable. But then, this is not, nor has it ever been, the *feminine* way of doing things. My response to my colleague simply suggested the other method. "Allow us (women from different cultures and traditions) time to *be* together," I said. "Let us give to one another our stories, and I trust that in our shared 'gospels' a common truth will emerge. From this we will work toward the humanization of the world."

The Unfreedom of One-sidedness

It must be stressed once again that the theological method I am describing is not *new* in the sense of "completely original." What I am calling the "feminine" mode of addressing the ultimate questions of existence has been with us since the beginning of time. We are, after all, all of us in the image of God relational beings. So women do not have exclusive ownership of this mode.

The confusion which has befallen the entire endeavor to speak meaningfully about the masculine and feminine polarities of existence has its source, as I see it, in a very complex social and historical structure in which for centuries male domination (caught in the Will to Power, as all domination invariably is) took hold of *one particular* mode of knowing — the one most conducive to the maintenance and stabilization of dominance — and excluded all other forms of approaching reality, calling them weak, inefficient, insufficient, and effeminate.

The hidden psychological reasons for this, pointing to the innate fear of encountering these traits within, which subsequently brought about the projection of stereotypes, cannot be discussed within the scope of this reflection. Ann Belford Ulanov in her book *Receiving Woman* does an excellent job identifying these issues.[5]

The oppression which ensued from this kind of exclusivism was global. Not only did anything feminine become the object of scorn, but the "feminine" potential in men, that is, the potential to receive and respond to the gift of the world in a manner of grateful creativity rather than of calculative certainty and dominance, was denied to men as well.

It has rightly been said of us in the Western hemisphere that we have become half-brained. The left hemisphere of the brain with its control over calculative thinking and accuracy has been honored in our temples of learning, while creative and passionate waiting for the emergence of truth from the depths of who we are has been viewed as poetic sentimentality — mere feeling, as weak, useless, unproductive, feminine. However, half-brained people are not whole and can never be holy. Half-sexed people (those who hold tenaciously to all their gender roles without allowing the contra-sexual within them to emerge) are not whole either. As Jung points out, human beings are called to spend most of the second half of life integrating the polarities of existence. He insists that unless we are willing to take the risk of letting go of the securities which firm entrenchment in one exclusive way of seeing life offers, we will never be whole; we will never be free; the wedding feast, as John Sanford describes it,[6] will never take place within us.

The right of the feminine to be heard in our age, then, does not arise primarily as a mandate of common decency and justice, but rather as a mandate toward wholeness. This mandate addresses men and women alike. Anyone can be caught in the Will to Power. The temptation of some women to do away with any and all gender differentiation and level all of humankind to one common denominator is just as problematic as the temptation of some men to "keep women in place," or the temptation of "justice-intoxicated" men to bring women up into their arenas of power.

The reason why this is so is that it denies the dialectic, the creative tension from which alone life can emerge and out of which nature speaks everywhere. Ulanov puts it well:

> Masculine and feminine poles act as central symbols in describing all of life's polarities. They give images and imaginative elaboration to the human experience of difference and otherness.[7]

Those of us familiar with logic know that contradictions "kill." They are exclusive and deny their opposites. Leveling or suppressing the feminine creates "contradictions." Coexistence as well as mutuality is denied. Polarities, on the other hand, open up to *rapprochement* even as they uphold differences. They avoid exclusion: the denying of one thing by the simple affirmation of its other. They further a new life, a fuller truth, a greater depth, by allowing for union even while upholding the dialectic.

The mandate toward a feminine spirituality comes from the male-female polarity *within us* that cries out toward liberation. We need to return ourselves to ourselves. The call comes from the beyond that is within us. It is a call to become who we are and warns us that the liberation of women *must* be the liberation of men as well, or it is not authentic.

The Home of Feminine Spirituality

By way of conclusion it may be well to reflect more directly upon some sources of feminine models of spirituality in our tradition. Interestingly enough, in my own search for these I have at times found myself attracted to symbols of God spoken *not* by women but by what Helen Caldicott calls "nurturent men." This can be explained, I think, by the fact not only that some "radical" feminine theology is caught in the "upward thrust" of a hierarchical system and, therefore, is not really radical enough but also that some men, often under great duress (they were officially condemned or forbidden to teach), have nurtured within themselves the contra-sexual openness to the world; that is, they have acknowledged the feminine within and have spoken from the depth where all of us are one.

Men and women who nurture rather than dissect the Holy have traditionally been identified as mystics. Their language speaks of the wholeness for which we are searching in this reflection. Dorothee Soelle puts it well in her foreword to *Beyond Mere Obedience*:

> Thus I set out to find a better theological language that could get rid of the streak of domination. I was helped by the language of the mystics. "Source of all that is good," "life-giving wind," "water of life," "light" are all symbols of God which do not imply power of authority and do not smack of any chauvinism. There is no room for "supreme power," domination, or the denial of one's own validity in the mystical tradition. It often explicitly criticizes the lord-servant relationship and it has been superseded particularly by the mystics' inventive use of language. In this tradition religion means the experience of being one with the whole, of belonging together, but never subjection. In this

perspective people do not worship God because of his power and domination. They rather want to "drown" themselves in God's love, which is the "ground" of their existence. There is a preference for symbols like "depth," "sea," and those referring to motherhood and to nature at large. Here our relationship to God is not . . . a matter of a distant God exacting sacrifice and self-denial, but rather a matter of agreement and consent, of being at one with what is alive. And this then becomes what religion is about.[8]

This becomes what spirituality is about: the flavor, the vision, the sound, the feel of our religious perspective; the ambience: that which allows us to see, to reflect on, to interpret the ultimate questions of our existence. It addresses, or rather, through it *we* address who for us is the ground of our being and what the nature of our response to this ground is, or ought to be. Through it's focus we interpret *call*; we experience truth; we embrace one another. Through it we also understand alienation and evil. From over-againstness we move to mutual affirmation; from domination and mandatory conformity we embrace the relational: we honor diversity even as we uphold community. From proclaiming independence, doing one's "own thing," we move to interdependence. The perspective that arises out of a confrontational attitude is obsessed with self-preservation and enhancement. The other, even if we are commanded to love him/her, is ultimately "hell," as Sartre so perceptively observed in his commentaries on the human condition. If we however stand in tender self-possession, releasement, in solidarity with others, poor and in vulnerable openness to all of life, we can give up the self; we can let-be; we can serve and we can wait for we belong to the universe and the universe belongs to us.

What has come to be known as the creation spirituality of Meister Eckhart,[9] and has been discussed in some detail at the beginning of this book, stands for me as one of the primary sources of this holistic way of encountering the Holy. Holistic symbols abound in Eckhart's writings, as they do in his Dominican foremother's, Mechthild of Magdeburg:

> We flow into God and God into us they both say. . . . Mechthild acknowledges humanity's divinity and divinization with the image of God's divinity flowing into us. Eckhart follows suit. Instead of conceiving of spiritual disciplines in terms of exercises of climbing up ladders, Mechthild invokes the gentler image of "sinking." So does Eckhart. Mechthild talks often of God as "fire" . . . within and without us. This image evokes Eckhart's use of the "inner spark" in each person, the source of creativity and the Holy Spirit. Mechthild, like Eckhart, talks of "melting" with divine life, of "bubbling over," of remaining young in the sense of "ever fresh and ever green," of returning to "the Source." . . . While Mechthild can talk about herself as male, Eckhart talks of himself as pregnant like a woman with child. Both Mechthild and Eckhart distrust asceticism but instead counsel "being still," "being quiet" and loving nothingness and darkness. Both invoke images of God as an underground river that floods over and springs up into the person who is "bare to himself or herself." . . . Both find the culmination in the spiritual journey not in a contemplative gazing at but in creativity and bearing fruit. . . . True emptying . . . leads to creative service, pouring out of compassion.[10]

Mechthild as well as Eckhart would in our day be classified as panentheists. For them, "we are in God and God in us."[11] This spirituality moves beyond dualism with its God "out there," or even the reverse: God merely "inside." The holistic spirituality for which they stand is in touch with feeling but far removed from any saccharine form of sentimentalism. It's passion speaks of com-passion. It is active in building the Kingdom and healing a broken and bleeding humanity.

There is, therefore, nothing weak in this spirituality. It speaks of self-emptying, not out of fear of self-containedness, but in radical response to the Gospel.[12] We empty ourselves in order to become ourselves. It speaks of stillness, not because it advocates mindless tranquility, but rather out of an urgent need to *hear*, to listen, and creatively to stand in the question of existence. We live in the fullness of time, as Donald Nicholl tells us.[13] Our primary task is creative gratitude. In coming home to ourselves as open receptivity we return God to Him/Herself. This is no task for trembling knees and weak hearts. The *fiat* of a Mother of God is meant for the strong. Within the world view of our time, of course, we have a tendency to forget this. Ulanov points this out powerfully when she writes about Mary:

> Rarely in liturgical worship do we celebrate Mary as a figure of fierce aggressive capacities who singly held herself open to God's presence, without support of reason or conventions of her culture. Only another female, Elizabeth, who found herself in an almost equally anomalous position, gave Mary company.[14]

In our view of Mary, and analogously of our own call to virgin motherhood, we have almost unanimously ignored the contrasexual wholeness which comprised the makeup of the Mother of God. We ignore it in her; we ignore it in ourselves. We forget that the Will to Power which we so frequently mistake for strength points rather to one-sidedness and insecurity. Paradoxically, the will to surrender holds within itself courage and creative energy. The Will to Power speaks of divisiveness and subservience. It is the forget-fulness of God. The will to surrender returns us to the truth of our being and brings us to wholeness. Surrender to the Holy dwells in remembrance of our heritage, our home in God, and inspires thankfulness.

Why is it necessary today to move toward a feminine spirituality? Because the time is ripe. In these days of alienation when mind without heart, calculation without passion, is driving us ever farther away from our center, we need to recognize the polarities in which we stand and come home to ourselves. The time is ripe for mothering. We are called to bear the diversity of the Holy within ourselves in courage and in love. We are called in gratitude to bear God back to God.

Notes

1. Beatrice Bruteau, "Neo-Feminism and the Next Revolution of Consciousness," *Anima* 3/2 (Spring 1977):3.

2. Heraclitus, Fragment 60.

3. Martin Heidegger, *Holzwege*, 4th ed. (Frankfurt am Main: Vittorio Klostermann, 1963), p. 200.

4. Dorothee Soelle, *Beyond Mere Obedience*, trans. Lawrence W. Denef (New York: Pilgrim Press, 1982), pp. xvi, xvii.

5. Ann Belford Ulanov, *Receiving Woman* (Philadelphia: Westminster Press, 1981), chap. 3.

6. John A. Sanford, *The Kingdom Within* (New York: Paulist Press, 1970), chap. 10.

7. Ulanov, *Receiving Woman*, p. 35.

8. Soelle, *Beyond Mere Obedience*, p. xix, xx.

9. Matthew Fox, *Original Blessing* (Santa Fe, N.M.: Bear and Company, 1983). This book summarizes Eckhart's spirituality simply and comprehensively for the English reader. Although Fox has written about it in several works previous to this, this is his latest discussion of Eckhart. See espec. also his *Breakthrough* (Garden City, N.Y.: Doubleday, 1980).

10. Sue Woodruff, *Meditations with Mechthild of Magdeburg* (Santa Fe, N.M.: Bear and Company, 1982), p. 9.

11. Ibid.

12. Mark 8:34–38.

13. Donald Nicholl, *Holiness* (New York: Seabury Press, 1981), pp. 14–19.

14. Ulanov, *Receiving Woman*, pp. 35, 36.

7

Androgynous Ministry:
A Call to Conversion

A conversion rarely happens unannounced. In the beginning of the previous chapter I suggested that it would take nothing short of a revolution of consciousness, a conversion, to move us from our estrangement from mystery toward an authentic appropriation of ourselves. The movements of this conversion, I believe, are emerging among us. They do not address us in isolation as unrelated moments detached from the flow of our lives. They light up in a fourfold event of ongoing retrieval through which we are regrounded, rooted as it were, into our call to authenticity and moved toward ever greater creativity.

The fourfold event of conversion can be described as: (1) *The preliminary experience of disorientation*. One experiences a deterioration, if you will, of previous levels of awareness, previous attitudes. There is a sense of alienation from what has hitherto been taken for granted. (2) *A moment of crisis*. The deterioration moves to a climax. Alienation reaches a fever pitch. One encounters a turning point where one either moves or is swallowed up. (3) *The moment of new insight*. A sudden breakthrough occurs. Revelation dawns upon the sufferer. There is new light, the end of the tunnel. (4) *The embracing of the revelation*. One says yes. One surrenders to the *New*. One's life is transformed. The insight affects one's entire way of being. There is a change in disposition, value orientation, action. Insight moves us toward radical depth. "When insight happens," Heidegger tells us, "we are struck in our *very being* by the lightning flash of Being. In insight we ourselves are gazed upon."[1] It is clear from the above that conversion is not something we effect, but something into which we are called and in the face of which even our response, though free, takes on the form of surrender-as-gift rather than planned execution.

Our times invite us to conversion. More specifically, they necessitate a turning from the dualistic divisiveness of our interactions, the over-againstness of our striving for control, toward authentic encounter. We are called in these days of relational indigence to embrace each other in our otherness and to find there our at-oneness, our unity. The title of this chapter, "Androgynous Ministry: A Call to Conversion," states this explicitly, for the androgyny holds within him/her the sacredness of the contra-sexual and thus radically symbolizes the polarities of existence, the human experience of diversity and otherness.

Not all of us are equally aware of the need for conversion toward androgyny to which the evolution of spirituality is calling us. The movements of conversion as I pointed out above emerge out of the flow of our lives. We are beings on the way, hence in different places as we journey into depth. Some of us may simply be sensing a global deterioration, an "existential frustration," as Victor Frankl would call it,[2] but we may not as yet know how or where to address it. We may be slowly becoming aware that spirituality as it has been conceived and preached up to now simply no longer "washes." We observe ourselves speaking of justice and love for all humankind, but somehow it seems that these words have no integrity. We may feel that as Church we might be clinging too tightly to what is already slipping through our fingers and we wonder why we hold on with such tenacity.

For others among us the moment of crisis and confusion has arrived. We are angry. Our anger might be directed at the Church and social structures generally for not addressing the issue properly. On the other hand, we might be enraged with women for disturbing the peace with semantics. Anger may easily cause us to react negatively. We become "hard-core." Either we stereotype even more blindly than before—call all women "hysterical" or see all men as "power hungry tyrants"— or we deny all differences and preach a bland and stubborn type of sameness.

Crisis, however, is the call to turn and to open ourselves up to a different perspective. We are invited to stand in the pain of our confusion, to endure the rage so that new insight may be given us. And this is where still others among us are. It is not necessarily a pleasant experience to stand in the event of recep-tive waiting, to receive the new and to surrender to it. The call to conversion rarely is pleasant. To embrace the mandate for an androgynous attitude, for an androgynous way of seeing the world and of working for the reign of God, is a frightening business. It must address culturally engrained attitudes, thou-sands of years of overagainstness instead of mutuality. It must face deep, often unconscious presuppositions: "what is male is not only different, but better." We must allow ourselves to en-counter fears. These always befall us when we know that we are facing the radically other. We must accept uncertainty as to where all of this will lead us; with uncertainty there is the dread of risk.

There is, if you will, a *birthing* going on in many of us along with all the horror and fear that overcomes the baby as it leaves one form of knowing the world and moves into the frighteningly unknown. There is also a dying to previous ways of acting and responding and a yes to radically *inclusive* percep-tions and responses. All of this may appear quite exciting to the uninitiated eye, but most of us have lived long enough to know the pain of authentic surrender, when theory is put into prac-tice.

The task of this chapter's reflection is to probe the depth of conversion into which the "gender crisis" of our time is calling us as ministers and to explore some possibilities of how one might realistically start to minister out of this depth dimension toward androgyny.

Difficulties with the Concept

To begin with, it will be important to note that the concept "androgyny" poses some difficulties. It runs the risk of reductionism. As Ulanov observes, it professes to "free us" from sexual stereotyping. It pictures the whole person as a *blend* of masculine and feminine characteristics. It emphasizes the role of cultural conditioning in forming gender identity."[3] Though all of this may seem very appealing to begin with, it can lead to extremes. We all know the injustice which can flow from the acceptance of such slogans as "anatomy is destiny." The absolutization of environmental influences does not guarantee anything better.

The danger lies in ignoring the concrete reality of our bodies as different in their male and femaleness. Because they are the place, the *locus*, through which we live in this world, they will influence the *how* of our manner of living. Ulanov puts it well and strikes a fine balance when she points out that

> The body houses the spiritual, physical, psychological forces through which and by which we touch other people and are touched by them. Our body space does affect and shape us; but it *does not altogether determine us*. Our particular psyches, cultural backgrounds, and large symbolic inheritances of masculine and feminine images influence us decisively.[4]

The body, the psyche, and culture all exert formative influences on our self-image. What we cannot forget is that cultural images in themselves can be changed by conscious intervention, but the consciousness that intervenes is one filled and formed

by the very images it is altering. "These images are created by
the interplay of personal and social life, by inherited instinct
and custom, by conscious and unconscious worlds of experience."[5] Androgyny, therefore, which intermingles the masculine and the feminine into a blend that acknowledges neither is
too simplistic. To quote Ulanov once more:

> If we adopt the image of androgyny as a literal description of
> human sexuality, we are almost bound to flee the concrete tasks
> of learning to live as men and women, to differentiate conflict-
> ing images within us, to integrate instinctual drives, and to
> harmonize the symbols that insist on proclaiming the masculine
> and feminine sides of ourselves.[6]

As ministers of the Gospel (the story of God-among-us), it
would be dangerous to succumb to this simplistic solution of
the gender crisis. Whereas it is clearly our task to respond to
the injustice of sexism, it is doubtful that we will achieve anything if we deny sexual differentiation. We know that biologi-
cally life blossoms forth in the union of the different. I suggest
that life within, movement toward the whole, integrity, can also
be brought about only through a union of the opposites within
us. It is not achieved through a denial of these opposites. (This,
if nothing else, is a form of violence to the body as the home of
our being.) It is achieved through the naming and embracing of
them, through a holding of these opposites in creative tension,
through a letting them *be*, letting them manifest themselves.

Sexism and Stereotypes

It is interesting to note that the sin of sexism in our time is
really not so much the affirmation of sexual differentiation as it
is the *suppression of one sexual identity at the* (unconscious) *expense of
the other*: a man is *only* a man. He cringes at anything feminine

within him seeing it as demeaning, unacceptable, weak and in need of suppression. A woman, on the other hand, can only succeed in the *real* world to the extent to which she adopts masculine qualities (while, at the same time, in order to remain attractive to men, she always of course has to "appear" feminine). The "really" real world, however, is masculine and a woman's success will depend on how truly masculine she can be without showing it. Because reality as a whole is masculine, so is God. Woman is merely a "presence" to assuage loneliness and to silence the body and its urges—the only dimension of our being that cannot lie, cannot rationalize away its own inherent affirmation of the different. It seems quite probable that it is because our body is virtually "shouting" out in dismay at its unjustified isolation in this matter, that body differentiation has become so exaggerated and therefore so stereotypical and offensive in the market place. A quick glance at the cosmetic industry, at the Playboy mentality of the media and, generally, at consumer sex is sufficient to supply us with examples.

Now a stereotype is not a falsehood as much as it is an exaggerated one-sidedness. Perhaps the following example can clarify this. It is claimed that women are passive. We all know that for sexual orgasm the element of "passivity"—relaxation—is to some extent necessary for women, just as a certain "aggressivity"—urgency—is necessary for men. Somehow, however, we jump to a generalization and claim that *all* women are therefore passive. We then proceed to associate this with "weak" and "helpless." Passivity thus becomes a negative quality by the very fact that women exhibit it under certain circumstances during which men generally do not. It follows according to the laws of sexism that men may therefore not be passive. They *ought* not show this trait, at least not if they wish to be "real" men. In all of this it seems to have been forgotten that a woman's sexual passivity in its totality goes far beyond mere dependency and inertia. There is something highly active and creative in nurturing a child in the womb and, for that matter, in the self-gift which is surrender in love. There is something daring, "aggressive," deeply charged in the act of cocreation. Once again we might want to reflect on the words of Ulanov cited in the previous chapter concerning the *fiat* of the Mother of God.

The exaggeration and absurdity which is highlighted once we identify a stereotype frequently provoke a reaction in kind. We are tempted to respond to it by denying, or, at least, feeling that we "should" deny, the quality which the stereotype has distorted. This is a mistake often made by feminists today. To return to our example: it is important to note that one ought not deny passivity to women when one discovers that passivity has become a "stereotype." What one *ought* to deny is feminine exclusivity to this quality or masculine exclusivity to its opposite. In this way one frees it; one releases it. Men, then, can claim it as theirs without feeling "less like men." Women can allow themselves to feel assertive in their loving and in their day-to-day interactions without feeling ashamed or out of place.

A female colleague of mine once exclaimed to me in sheer desperation concerning this stereotype: "When you or I get angry we are 'aggressive,' 'out of place,' and we even feel the need to mend our ways, and apologize. When men get angry, on the other hand, they are simply 'assertive'—a commendable quality." With the identification and subsequent claiming of stereotypes this situation could be balanced out: women have a right to assert themselves (as do men) when they face an unjust situation. Inappropriate aggressivity befits neither. Here again, however, it is important to realize that to allow women to be assertive without labeling them "emasculated" or "out of place," and to allow men to be creatively passive (as is the writer, the musician, the artist, the tender lover) without accusing them of being effeminate is not to level them to a common denominator. Men will be passive out of their embodied and psychic being. Women will be assertive out of theirs. Passivity, in other words, will be nuanced by maleness; assertiveness, by femaleness. Neither gender has the prerogative to what "real" or "healthy" aggressivity or passivity is.

Reality as Androgynous

It is out of this understanding that it becomes possible to see reality generally as androgynous. By this is meant that all of it belongs to humankind and was released to us for our shepherding. Its diversity in all its fullness was created, and continues to be created, for and through man *and* woman as the image of God, as the channels of meaning.

The divine image as male *and* female is still too frequently shunned in favor of the second creation account in which the woman, as helpmate formed from man, receives for us a subordinate position. In this regard it may be of interest to refer the reader to June Singer's discovery concerning the etymology of the word *Elohim* in the first creation account. While researching the history of androgyny she happened upon S. L. MacGregor Mathers's book *The Kabbalah Unveiled*, and there read how Mathers's curiosity had been aroused by the strange wording in the first creation story: God created man in his image *male and female*. God, then blessed *them* and ordered *them* to be fruitful. In her account of this Singer observes that it puzzled Mathers how "for some reason . . . the translators of the Bible have carefully crowded out of existence and smothered every reference to the fact that the deity is both masculine *and* feminine."[7] She quotes Mathers directly:

> They have translated a *feminine plural* by a *masculine singular* in the case of the word Elohim. They have, however, left an inadvertent admission of their knowledge that it was plural in Gen. iv. 26; "And Elohim said: Let Us make man." Again (v. 27), how could Adam be made in the image of Elohim, male and female, unless the Elohim were male and female also?[8]

We have in this account a profoundly significant example of the suppression of the feminine and the subsequent identification of reality as male rather than an acceptance of it as androgynous. It is an example of the impoverishment of all creation by the denial of the contra-sexual. If God's diversity breaks out in all of creation, as the mystics tell us, and if we are to be its proclaimers, then what are we doing by restricting it so but violating the Holy. By doing this, we violate ourselves as well.

> The word Elohim is plural formed from the feminine singular, *Eloh*, by adding IM to the word. But inasmuch as IM is usually the termination of the masculine plural, and is here added to a feminine noun, it gives to the word Elohim the sense of a female potency united to a masculine idea, and thereby capable of producing an offspring. Now we hear much of the Father and Son, but we hear nothing of the Mother in the ordinary religions of the day. But in the Qabalah we find that the Ancient of Days conforms Himself simultaneously into the Father and the Mother, and thus begets the Son. . . . Now we find that before the Deity conformed Himself thus—i.e., as male and female—that the worlds of the universe could not subsist, or, in the words of Genesis, "the earth was formless and void."[9]

Meditating on the creative energy which radiates toward us from this Hebrew understanding of the dynamism of God we ought to be saddened by its loss to us through the ages. Edward Hoffman in his book *The Way of Splendor: Jewish Mysticism and Modern Psychology* confirms my suspicion that the lifelessness and lack of enthusiasm which characterizes so much of contemporary religious practice may well be due to its one-sided and exclusivistic intentionality. When half of reality—that is, half of the creative breakthrough of God is ignored in our worship— what else can religion be but barren? Hoffman agrees with the Kabbalists that

> A major cause of the decline of impassioned Jewish religious belief and worship is precisely due to this elimination of femi-

nine images and symbols from day-to-day practices—leaving a more barren, masculine repository of values. Strikingly in recent years a variety of books in a related vein have argued that the modern, mainstream Judeo-Christian systems have indeed cut themselves off from an androgynous or sexually balanced approach to the transcendent.[10]

In Jungian terms, our churches have lost their anima or, perhaps more correctly put, they have so repressed her that she has in many cases turned negative.[11] Instead of being a trusted ally and friend, leading them to inwardness and wholeness, she now haunts them with practices of sentimental religiosity and thoughtless emotionalism that lack the energy both to act and to suffer for the sake of the Gospel. She holds them captive in the neurotic insecurities of legalism and protectionism that pretend to preserve values which have long lost their meaning due to the intellectual game playing and the rationalizations which now surround them.

The stubborn resistance to the ordination of women which uses nothing less than Scripture and tradition (misinterpreted though these may be) to justify itself, is probably the clearest example of the repressed feminine now turned sour. As such it is projected outward and inflicted on women whose rightful concerns are scorned as "senseless" and "radical," springing from "insecurity" and "touchiness." Little do the projectors realize that irritability, uncertainty, insecurity, touchiness, and sentimentalism are all symptoms of their own ignored anima.[12] These traits are the results of the denial and exclusion of the contra-sexual within the personality (in this case the male personality or the corporate personality of any exclusively male institution such as are many of our churches).

When, as in the Roman Catholic Church, men start sending out decrees concerning the ingredients for eucharistic bread and, in an attempt to maintain "tradition," stubbornly insist that the staple of colonial rulers be used for worship in nations where bread and wine must be imported at considerable expense, one can safely suspect that a repressed anima is wreaking havoc through legalism and intellectual game playing. Only an acknowledgment of the contra-sexual will give the Church back her "soul," as Jung would put it. Only the recognition of extreme one-sidedness can have us come to grips with our need for the other which cries out from within us to be heard and to help restore balance and some semblance of common sense. Jung warns us, however, that the animus-anima archetypal character structure within each of us can be brought to light in a fruitful and creative way only through successful interaction with persons of the other sex. Only then can projections be recognized and withdrawn. This task will be somewhat difficult, if not impossible, to accomplish in a virtually all-male Church.

Androgynous Ministry

The call toward androgynous ministry in our times is a call home from sterile one-sidedness and rigidity toward the affirmation of life and enthusiasm (Greek *en-theos*; "being possessed by God)," toward embracing our God in the sense of *Elohim* discussed above. We are therefore called to retrieve the contra-sexual as sacred, as the ground from which the "whole" can rise and holiness can be born. "Androginity is the ultimate union of male and female in a higher God-like being, the ultimate conquest of decadence and strife, the restoration . . . of the image and likeness of God."[13]

The primary division in a human being (hence in a culture and in a Church) is the masculine-feminine division.[14] Our primary task then is to work toward healing. Several points need to be made in this regard. It seems to me fundamental that the "androgynous minister" has to be preceded by the "androgynous person." By this I mean that disposition must precede action. How we minister is directly influenced by how we perceive and relate to the reality around us. In a male-dominated world the importance of the feminine must not just be conceded but must be valued both by men and by women. This means, therefore, that each one of us has to *dare* (and I mean this quite literally for it may be a very painful business for some of us) to encounter the other within and ultimately to embrace this other in a psychic marriage.

A discussion on the intricacies of this encounter would take us too deeply into Jung's theory of individuation[15] and is therefore beyond the scope of our reflection. Suffice it to say that for most of those who dare to move beyond their immediately given selves and to embrace the other within, the deepest moments of anguish and greatest moments of truth usually occur during what Jung has come to call the second half of life — mid-life and thereafter. Our reflections at the beginning of this chapter concerning the nature of crisis can certainly apply to this period of a person's life, as does our discussion on pain in chapter four, for it is an event of unquestionable grace, but also often one of great agony. The experience of conversion which addresses us at that time is indeed a turning point at the inner-most core of our being.

For the androgynous person, and, I would say, even for those of us who are still merely aspiring toward the integration of androgyny because we have come to see its necessity, it would seem to be a task of the greatest urgency to minister toward a broadening of consciousness, toward cultural integrity and ecclesial holiness. What are our realistic possibilities? My suggestion is threefold.

For those among us who profess relative comfort with the contra-sexual in our lives, I propose an all-out effort in our individual ministries to include persons from the opposing sex, not only "into our circle" but also into the decision-making positions of our ministries where we can then learn to be mutually supportive as well as challenging.

For those men who feel the need still to grow in an appreciation of the other in their lives, I recommend a conscious choice to work with women, to be taught by women, to seek out women as spiritual directors and counselors. Only through encounter with the contra-sexual person can one be led to face one's own inner partner.

I encourage women ministers to face honestly their anger, to name it, and then move beyond it. Becoming aware of personal and societal "put-downs" and differentiating these from honest and well-deserved criticism are essential for us. We need to become open in our communication, check perceptions, and accept advice and empowerment from each other. We also need to appreciate the honest efforts at inclusion made by our fellow male ministers.

Movement toward androgyny will take place not through inimical confrontation, but through patient transformation. Androgyny stands for dynamic relationship, for energy flowing from the union of the different. Though we have used the term "revolution of consciousness," we do not mean by revolution an "overthrow"; what Beatrice Bruteau identifies as "a mere coup d'etat whereby one set of rules is replaced by another set while the structure of ruling itself remains basically the same."[16] The androgynous way of seeing reality will not give women precedence over men. This would simply mean a change from oppressed to oppressor and is what generally follows a successful rebellion. It marks no change from one's enthrallment with the Will to Power. It speaks of overpowering rather than empowering and furthers neither growth nor freedom. "A genuine revolution must be a gestalt shift in the whole way of seeing our relations to one another so that our behavior patterns are reformed from the inside out."[17]

The suggestions which I have made for our ministerial endeavors, therefore, are suggestions that point more toward gestation than abrupt reform. No earth-shaking changes will be effected by them overnight. In working with and learning from each other, in interaction and dialogue that is open and honest, we will learn to *be* with each other. We will learn to ex-sist: stand beyond ourselves and toward one another; to "com-pan-ion" each other, that is, "break bread with" one another and slowly grow with and into each other, until the day when androgyny will emerge from the womb of our receptive-response to one another and we will have become the mirrors in which Elohim breaks forth.

Notes

1. Martin Heidegger, *Die Kehre*, Opuscula I (Pfullingen: Verlag Günther Neske, 1962), p. 45. The translation is mine and rendered loosely for the sake of inclusive language, the first person plural replacing the German *Mensch* normally translated as "man" or "men."

2. Victor Frankl, *The Unheard Cry for Meaning* (New York: Touchstone Books, 1978), p. 23.

3. Ann B. Ulanov, *Receiving Woman* (Philadelphia: Westminster Press, 1981), p. 49.

4. Ibid. (italics mine).

5. Ibid.

6. Ibid., p. 51.

7. June Singer, *Androgyny: Toward a New Theory of Sexuality* (Garden City, N.Y.: Anchor Books, 1977), p. 84.

8. Ibid.

9. Ibid., pp. 84, 85.

10. Edward Hoffman, *The Way of Splendor* (Boulder: Shambhala Publications, 1981), p. 81.

11. According to Jung the *anima* is the unconscious feminine dimension in a man. The *animus* is the unconscious masculine dimension in a woman. When acknowledged and reconciled, both anima and animus are extremely valuable psychic forces toward individuation and wholeness. If ignored or repressed, however, they become inimical and destructive. To the extent to which they are unnoticed

they are frequently projected outward: the anima into a woman and the animus into a man.

12. Carl G. Jung, 3rd ed., *Man and His Symbols* (Garden City, N.Y.: Doubleday and Company, 1964), pp. 178–80.

13. John A. Sanford, *The Kingdom Within* (New York: Paulist Press, 1970), p. 209. Sanford here is quoting Berdyaev in *The Meaning of the Creative Act*.

14. Ibid., p. 207.

15. I refer the interested reader particularly to works by Jung himself, by Emma Jung, his wife, by June Singer, Jolande Jacobe, Aniela Jaffé, Morton T. Kelsey, and John A. Sanford.

16. Beatrice Bruteau, "Neo-Feminism and the Next Revolution of Consciousness," *Anima* 3/2 (Spring 1977):3.

17. Ibid.

8

Prayer as Listening:
A Practical Approach

Preceding reflections addressed a variety of topics which, it seemed, presented particular concerns for us in our times: the nature of freedom, of obedience and authority; the call to solidarity with the poor; the paradox of pain; the problem of dualism in our culture, resulting in one-sidedness of perceptions and valuations and leading to insecurity, oppression, and an acceleration of the Will to Power. I did not approach these topics with a problem-solving attitude, however. My intention was to explore the phenomenon within each particular concern as it lights up for us in contemporary society — to probe its depth with the hope of finding a new way of dwelling in its presence. My stress then has been on *disposition*; my theme, *releasement*: receptive-responsive openness without the need to control or manipulate. My hope has been to invite the reader to see, to draw near to the issues, to become immersed in them and to live into their unfolding rather than to objectify them in order to *do* something with them or about them.

Though perhaps initially the impression, my approach does not spring from an undue preference for passivity. It originates, rather, in the conviction, stated over and over again in these chapters, that any activity which is not grounded in releasement is in fact ground-less. Unless we thought-fully and reverently hold ourselves within the diversity of everything that is, *as it is,* our actions will unquestionably succumb to the Will to Power and, in one way or other, we will do violence both to ourselves and to others. Our times are replete with examples of this. It is a difficult challenge to stand patiently in the questions of contemporary existence and allow them to unfold without imposing answers — solutions more often originating in our own need for security than in the courageous choice to wait and to let-be. Few are able to meet this challenge. I am convinced, however, that our call to holiness consistently invites us to face it and embrace it.

But how can one endure such waiting? How is such patience possible? I am tempted to invoke the Gospel response about the rich young man and say: "Things that are impossible for us *are* possible for God" (Luke 18:27; emphasis mine). To respond authentically to the challenge of these pages, therefore, it is paramount that ministers pray. But here, once again, we will need to face the activist's temptation of wanting to claim the services we render for our prayer, or of spending our moments of solitude so filled with chatter about the needs of our ministry that our inner temples become a "den of thieves."

> Whenever you pray, go to your room, close your door, and pray to your Father in private. Then your Father, who sees what no human sees, will repay you. In your prayer do not rattle on like the pagans. They think they will win a hearing by the sheer multiplication of words. Do not imitate them. Your Father knows what you need before you ask him. (Matt. 6:6–9)

Our prayer should be the time when the stillness of waiting is learned. It is the time for our apprenticeship in the art of releasement. A good friend of mine once put it wisely. "We must pray every day," she said, "so that every day may be prayer."

To learn the art of waiting we must, quite simply, practice the "presence of God." In our silent listening to the depth within, we will paradoxically be moved outward and beyond ourselves and begin to discover the world as the breakthrough of God. Prayer is not a separation from the world. Such concepts have validity only in the dualistic paradigm of over-againstness, insecurity and fear. Prayer *immerses us in the world* because it empowers us to see it with the eyes of freedom, as children of God, in creative surrender to the mystery which unfolds itself in its diversity and for our affirmation. In prayer we *learn* to listen instead of talk. Dispositions are acquired in silent attentiveness and humility. Just as we can love only because we have first been loved, so we can speak (respond authentically) only because we have first listened.

Prayer as Listening

A reflection upon the nature of prayer as listening will of necessity divide itself into two questions: What do we mean by prayer? What is understood by listening? Only after adequate consideration has been given to these issues will it be possible to discuss the *manner* of prayer, that is, the method whereby this prayer may be achieved.

Much has been written on the meaning of prayer and it is not the place here either to summarize, or critically to evaluate the treasures of the past. My aim is to go immediately to the heart of the matter and to expose the reader to the end so that his/her thirst for it will make the beginning all the easier.

Prayer, as I see it, is the response within us urging us toward union. It is a response which is, as it were, an echo reverberating within the depth of our own openness to God, calling us home to what the mystic Eckhart calls true "poverty of spirit,"[1] and interprets as a freedom not *from* things *for* God, but rather *of* God: divine freedom. This union is brought about when the experience of openness *to* God, noble as this may be, is *replaced* (for in the *to* there is still separation). In authentic prayer we *break out* of all these concepts and *know* that God and we are one. We, the creatures, become in prayer, as it were, "what we were before we were"; we sense ourselves as one with the divine; our prayer *is* union.[2] There is in the prayer of union no longer a willing on our part, for to will union presupposes a lack of it. The person of prayer *is* union. S/he does not strive for knowledge of divine things; rather, s/he abides in them. The "response," therefore, which *is* prayer is not an act *initiated* by us. That is why I referred to it above as an "echo." In authentic prayer all subject-object distinctions disappear and in the encounter of what, quite clearly, is no-thingness the human being experiences what might simply be called divine at-oneness.

The question which quite naturally flows from what has been discussed so far is: How does all this happen? This brings us to a consideration of listening, for if the prayer of listening is indeed the prayer of union, then it is in listening that it distinguishes itself from other forms of prayer in themselves such as petition, discursive meditation, liturgical worship of all kinds, and so on.[3]

Little reflection is needed to acknowledge that the essential characteristic of listening must be silence. By silence is meant that stillness within which one surrenders to the other and is alone capable (free from personal prejudices and objectifications) of *hearing* him/her. Let me explain: the German philosopher-theologian Bernhard Welte in an excellent work on the philosophy of religion sees the prayer of stillness as the unmediated response to a greatness which surpasses all words.[4] In prayer I encounter a limit situation. I reach, as it were, the threshold of my own beyond—though still within myself (I am immanent-transcendence). My response can only be that of reverential silence. I let go of all things, names, concerns, concepts, and desires to conceptualize. I let go of the desire to "grasp" in words. In the words of Welte, the prayer-filled person "lets his/her possession of the world and his/her being possessed by the world sink to the ground. S/he allows drives and curiosity to grow still. S/he becomes rest and releasement."[5]

In prayer I surrender before the unspeakable and become wordless myself—possessed of stillness. My surrender, if one were to explain it as "progression," is indeed a turning *from* things, but it is never *just* that, for simultaneously it is a readiness *for*: an openness best expressed in the word *releasement*. Here the "setting free" can only be understood in the paradox of detached-involvement or, as Welte explains, "in an attitude that allows us to be free from the world and free in the world and free for the world."[6]

Releasement is "pure hearing which . . . does not hear some*thing* but rather is open and ready to hear all."[7] It is an openness that gathers all that has been scattered into a multitude of directions, all that has divided the world into myriad interests and has thus destroyed it. "The stillness of the gathering . . . which has brought itself together out of dispersion, has, in the power emanating from the silence of this gathering a positive relation to the whole world and existence."[8] It bears the fruit of authentic re-collection. This positive relation consists in a *letting-be*, a refusal to distort or manipulate and control. It is in silent harmony with all, hence it is not "world-less" but rather "world-free." In it creature and Creator are one—the distinction and therewith the category vanishes. "In the stillness of silent readiness all is gathered, the whole of the outside world, the whole of the inside world; everything breathes out into freedom wherein it is gathered."[9] In gathering the world as such, the stillness of releasement transcends it. It "falls with the whole world which it has gathered in its expanse into the nameless abyss above and beyond the whole world,"[10] and here in silent namelessness, in no-thingness, reverential stillness hears the divine and *dwells in God*.

A simple expression often used might depict it better than any of the above: "sunk in prayer"—beyond oneself yet most authentically in tune with oneself, hence in union with God. This is what the Gospel means when it tells us that "the kingdom of God is within" (Luke 17:21).

An existential union, an "identification with" the divine—

this *is* the prayer of listening. In it the person of prayer hears, recognizes, God not because s/he is like the Son but because s/he is *one with* the Son. As Eckhart says: "If you want to recognize God then it is not enough to be like the Son, rather you must yourself be the Son."[11]

Reaction to what has been said so far may well be frustration. How, one might wonder, is such union possible in the type of world in which we live? Noise is a given; silence almost nonexistent. The above may have been possible for Eckhart and the mystics, but contemplation for persons of action seems near impossible most of the time.

The matter becomes *disturbing*, however, once we look deeper than our frustration and we are struck by the insight that what has been discussed is *not* a luxury for the few but an *existential necessity* for us all. Augustine tells us that our hearts are restless *until* they find their home in God. Eckhart stresses our oneness with God not only as essential for us but indeed, though in a different sense, as essentially God's.[12] Teilhard de Chardin says similar things and, in the Epistles, Paul exhorts us that the path to union is ceaseless prayer (1 Thess. 5:17).

The dilemma of our time is *not* that we do not have *time* to pray, rather *our prayerlessness causes the dilemma*. This is the age of nihilism, of alienation, not because God is dead but because the human person *as* human (as conscious articulation of creation *as* creation, hence of Creator) is dead. The microcosm, the image of the uni-verse, who holds within him/herself the voice of the spheres as a gift to be shepherded in prayer is dead. Our own will has fragmented us. We are atomized; have lost our oneness with the One and *will* our *own* oneness. Thus we desecrate the universe and cause disharmony in the midst of harmony.[13]

The call to prayer in our age, frustrating though our circumstances may be, is a call to existence. It summons us to ourselves. It gives us no choice: become who you are, or perish! How, then, can we learn to respond to God's invitation to

prayer? How can we learn to pray? Quite practically and in line
with what has been discussed above, we learn to pray by learning to be still, so that we can hear the breath of the Spirit. We
learn stillness through the age-old techniques of centering.[14] It
is quite clear that the world has so permeated our being, that
even a soundproof, distraction-free room will not liberate us
from the noise within. Grace *alone* will, and the surrender to
inwardness *springing* from grace.

A Method

Much, I am sure, has been said in the ancient traditions concerning the process of centering and the emptying of the mind.
One very simple method accessible to all is the following:

1. Choose a time and place. The length of time is best
    around thirty minutes; the place, private and undis-
    turbed.
2. Place yourself into the overwhelming presence of God
    and ask Him/Her in the name of Jesus to take posses-
    sion of every fiber of your being. Thank Him/Her for
    doing so, for every prayer uttered in the name of Jesus
    is answered.
3. Read a brief passage from Scripture — one or two vers-
    es — reminding you of the divine light illuminating
    your being.

Sit in a comfortable manner before an *icon*. The icon should
be at the level of your eyes. After 1, 2, and 3 above are complet-
ed, you gaze upon the icon. Breathe gently, slowly, normally.
Attempt neither physically nor intellectually to strain yourself.
It will help consciously to give your eyes and ears to the will of
God. Be present before Him/Her with a watchful and serene
heart.

Some clarification is necessary here concerning the word *icon*. Linda Sabbath in her forthcoming book dealing with the prayer of listening tells us that "the Eastern Orthodox icon has long been used by Eastern Christians to open the inward eyes to gaze into the essence and being of God."[15] Further, she says:

> The icon is a powerful revealed image of man's call to sanctification in visual, just as Scriptures are the powerful revealed image of his call in written, form. As the Buddhist monk employs his kasina and the Hindu yogin uses his mandala, gazing upon the icon initiates the gift of sight, the opening of inner eyes to see in and through the icon into the depths of God's being, into the essence of love.[16]

The veneration of the icon through the ordinance of the Seventh Ecumenical Council (Nicaea II, 787) was placed on a level with the cross and the Gospels. Hereby a correspondence was established between word and image. In the image of the icon the Word of God becomes present.[17]

When one is introduced to the method of prayer mentioned above, four images are presented respectively: (1) a square shaped paper of mellow color serves as the background to a crucifix. One gazes upon the mystery of one's faith: God becomes human and is crucified for our sins. (2) The second image presents the cross without the Corpus, and one is led to reflect upon the Mystical Body: "With Christ I am nailed to the Cross" (Gal. 2:19). (3) The third image is the square-shaped paper. Its center now bears the cross with a round mirror at the center. The message given already is intensified, for in gazing upon this icon one now sees oneself: "Continually we carry about in our bodies the dying of Jesus, so that in our bodies the life of Jesus may also be revealed" (2 Cor. 4:10). (4) Finally, the square-shaped paper with the golden center (the personal icon) is presented. One is invited to gaze upon it and respond in silent surrender and openness. "For God who said, 'Let light

1

2

3

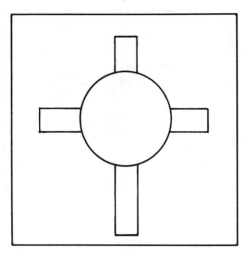

4

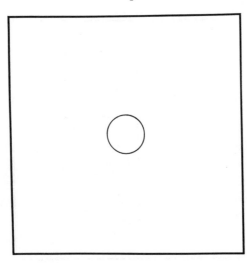

shine out of darkness,' has shone in our hearts, that we in turn might make known the glory of God shining on the face of Christ. This treasure we possess in earthen vessels, to make it clear that its surpassing power comes from God and not from us" (2 Cor. 4:6, 7).

The icon, a simple device to further inwardness, is blessed before its use and, it must be stressed once more, this entire approach to the prayer of listening is preceded by a reading from Scripture. One consciously places oneself into the presence of God and surrenders to Him/Her.

Should we choose this method of prayer, our minds will quite naturally enter a deeper state of consciousness. Silence will befall us, and should distractions beset us, a gentle return of the heart (devoid of all upset concerning our lack of "concentration") will restore our peace.

Given our being as embodied spirit, our deeper state of consciousness may quite likely bring with it unfamiliar sensory stimulation. We will relax and at times muscles will twitch or parts of our bodies feel heavy. Our eyes, no longer under the control of voluntary perception, may be opened to colors and perceptions not usually given to the conscious mind. None of this should in any way prove disturbing to us, though, having been used to left hemisphere control of our sensory input (which categorizes and conceptualizes all perception), this new surrender to deeper involuntary vision may at first prove puzzling.

The question that should be asked at this point is: And what of prayer? *Prayer occurs when our own will surrenders to the will of God.* The physiological responses described above are obviously not prayer in themselves. We will soon discover that distractions, which at first would dissipate any involuntary perception of the senses, can, after a while, quite easily happen to us simultaneously. All that this technique of centering our being brings about is the *possibility* for surrender, which in the usual distractions of everyday existence has become near impossible. Given the possibility for inner silence and openness, the yes will ever be *ours* — an ongoing process *initiated* and *nurtured by grace*.

Discernment

The person given to this "method" of prayer-filled silence will undoubtedly soon discover the difference between simple relaxation and authentic prayer. The New Testament teaches us to recognize deeds by their fruit. Prayer too is recognized that way. Growth in charity and the genuine feeling of goodwill put into practice in numerous ways are undoubtedly signs of progress toward union with the God who is Love. Others are the desire and ability to overcome temptation; a letting-be of what normally was clung to inordinately; the desire for the actual making of peace. A person who practices authentic prayer will feel the need for it and long for it. Time previously filled with the usual entertainment of TV, radio, and movies will for the prayerful person soon become a precious opportunity for union with God.

And what of visions and mystical experiences? Can involuntary sense perceptions ever be more than a neurological phenomenon? The answer is an unmitigated yes. When this occurs, the prayer-filled soul will know. Here is an example.

At the Thomas Merton Center for Contemplative Prayer in Quebec, Canada, a retreatant, perhaps best described as of "analytical faith" (accepting the possibility of mystical experience for everyone else but herself), was given an experience of what writers on contemplative prayer may quite simply refer to as "the divine light." She had practiced the prayer of listening off and on for about ten months before coming to the center, and had often, upon entering a deeper state of consciousness, seen vibrations of various colors: off-white, green, purple, and deep gold. The feeling of relaxation usually accompanied these experiences aside from the more prayerful experiences of peace and closeness to God.

The regular sittings at the center enhanced these experiences but distractions were not always absent and had to be dealt with gently and firmly. The Heart to Heart prayer[18] taught at the center intensified the white-gold light given to her from her icon. Then one evening she quite unexpectedly experienced the following (taken with permission from the journal of the retreatant):

> Have been since yesterday praying wordlessly for His/Her light to illuminate me, so that others and I might come to know His/Her love more deeply. [The retreatant's breath prayer, by that time quite internalized, was "Sear my heart and cleanse me, Lord.[19]]
>
> Prayed so during prayer of listening sittings. Colors were intense but mostly purple. Prayer got more silent toward evening and "love sickness" pains [a physical pain which the retreatant had experienced previously during a broken love affair and which had now returned with no "apparent" object present] came back just before Heart to Heart prayer sitting. I started it as usual: breath prayer, raising of sexual energy[20]—also using icon which gives off white-gold waves during Heart to Heart prayer—never yet during other sittings. All of a sudden I received an intense sting into the heart—to the point of reaching up to it. It took me a while to recover.
>
> Shortly after that the entire icon was illuminated with beautiful gold radiance. It went way beyond the icon and seemed to illuminate my entire corner and me. My head felt like bursting with intense energy. I was wondering what on earth was happening. I thought I was lit up too and kept saying: "I believe," "I believe," "I am yours." Then I felt a cool breeze over my face while the brilliance endured and I hoped it would never go away. I was stupified—wordless, and stayed that way for a long time after. Nothing has ever been like this! I felt healed.

A subsequent entry in the journal showed that she had felt a "replacement," as it were, of her heart by the divine light. Somehow her heart "was no longer." Its place was filled with the light of God. For days the silence pervading her being lasted.

She discovered that she found it easier to love people for whom she had previously experienced antipathy. She sensed that her heart was no longer free to dislike — as it was no longer hers, but had been seared by divine love and belonged to God.

Some neurologists without any interest in the spiritual dimension of the human person might quite easily have a field day with this experience. Would this really matter? We are embodied spirit. Our quest is *essentially* union with God. In this quest the intellect has often hindered us more than helped us, causing us to mistake knowledge *about* God for knowledge *of* God. We reach for other states of consciousness which facilitate surrender and union. In silence, with docile and open vision, we give ourselves to waiting for our God. We experience intense union and our lives are changed. "Inside or out of the body" we know not — but this we know: God is Love.

Another retreatant at the center quite simply had the inner vision of a painting, made several years previously, of herself. The immediate intuition that came to her during this experience was an intense certainty that this was the Lord. Seen without the eyes of prayer this would be narcissism — intense and inordinate self-glorification. Seen with the eyes of prayer, Eckhart's observation applies here:

> We are being totally transformed into God and changed into Him; in the same manner as in the Sacrament bread is changed into the Body of Christ: I am changed into Him in such a manner that He himself brings me forth as His being, as one, not (simply) as something like Him; before the living God it is true, there is no difference here.[21]

I have earlier quoted Eckhart insisting that for a knowledge, a recognition of God, the person of prayer must be transformed into the Son.[22] Contemplative prayer is "bold" prayer. As contemplatives we reclaim our birthright won back for us by Jesus Himself. Our boldness is no illusion, however. What, after all, have we been taught from Christ Himself? We have been urged to eat the meal of our fellowship in Christ, to break the bread of God-among-us. Food, given its natural function, becomes part of the one who consumes it. The believing Christian then is transformed *into* the son/daughter of God. What as contemplatives we see in prayerful vision (be it sensory, intellectual, or simply through intuitive knowledge) is our union in God. In prayer we become who we are. In listening we receive the affirmation of our sonship and daughterhood. We receive the glory won for us through the death and resurrection of Christ. What the intellect, through years of misplaced speculations has dimmed and even distorted, is given back to us in the certainty of humble surrender. We live in glory!

"I live now not I, but Christ lives in me."

Notes

1. Josef Quint, ed., *Meister Eckhart, Deutsche Predigten und Traktate* (Munich: Carl Hanser Verlag, 1963), Sermon 32, pp. 303–309 (trans. mine). Hereafter, Quint.

2. Quint, pp. 308, 309.

3. I hasten to point out here that when prayer *is* union it permeates all forms of prayer, and distinctions which may be necessary initially cease to exist.

4. Bernhard Welte, *Religionsphilosophie* (Freiburg im Breisgau: Herder Verlag, 1978), pp. 183, 184.

5. Ibid., p. 185 (inclusive language and trans. mine).

6. Bernhard Welte, *Meister Eckhart* (Freiburg: Herder, 1979), p. 176 (trans. mine).

7. Welte, *Religionsphilosophie*, p. 185 (italics mine).

8. Ibid.

9. Ibid., p. 186.

10. Ibid.

11. Quint, p. 227, Sermon 16.

12. Quint, pp. 251–55, Sermon 22. See also Welte, *Meister Eckhart*, pp. 223–26.

13. Welte, *Meister Eckhart*, pp. 223–26.

14. Please note that this word is used here *simply* to connote the turning inward in silent openness to the divine which is essential for all contemplative prayer. We are not referring to any particular form of prayer that uses this title.

15. Linda Sabbath, "The Prayer of Listening" (unpublished manuscript), p. 61.

16. Ibid., p. 7.

17. Ibid.

18. Linda Sabbath, *The Radiant Heart* (Denville, N.J.: Dimension Books, Inc., 1977), pp. 40–48.

19. Ibid. pp. 11–25, for an understanding of the breath prayer. Other writings refer to it as *mantra*: a seven syllable ejaculation said while breathing in and breathing out.

20. A centering of creative energy in the heart. See Ibid., pp. 26–39.

21. Quint., p. 451.

22. See no. 11 above.